GARAGE
CONVERSIONS

GARAGE CONVERSIONS

Planning, managing and completing your conversion

Laurie Williamson

THE CROWOOD PRESS

First published in 2006 by
The Crowood Press Ltd
Ramsbury, Marlborough
Wiltshire SN8 2HR

www.crowood.com

British Library Cataloguing-in-Publication Data
A catalogue record for this book is available from the British Library.

ISBN10   1 86126 874 2
ISBN13   978 1 86126 874 7

Disclaimer
The author and the publisher do not accept any responsibility, in any manner
whatsoever, for any error, or omission, nor any loss, damage, injury, adverse
outcome or liability of any kind incurred as a result of the use of any of the
information contained in this book, or reliance upon it. Readers are advised to
seek professional advice relating to their particular garage, house, project and
circumstances before embarking on any building or installation work.

All illustrations by the author.

Typeset in Melior by Bookcraft Ltd, Stroud, Gloucestershire

Printed and bound in Malaysia by Times Offset (M) Sdn Bhd

CONTENTS

About this book 7
Introduction 8

CHAPTER 1: MAKING PLANS 9

Site Survey 10
Planning Ahead 14
Planning Permission 15
Listed Building Consent 17
Integral Garage 19
Link-Attached Garage 19
Detached Garage 19
No Change 20
Building Regulations 21
Structural Survey 22

CHAPTER 2: INTERNAL PREPARATIONS 25

Preparing a Flow Chart 26
Additional Plans 26
Obtaining Quotations (Tradesmen) 29
Obtaining Quotations (Materials) 31
Value Added Tax (VAT) 31
Finding a Builder 32
Understanding Your Quotation 33
Payments 34
Ordering Materials 35
Safety and Insurance 36
Risk Assessments 36

CHAPTER 3: EXTERNAL PREPARATIONS 38

Storing Materials 38
Room to Work 40
Plant and Equipment Hire 41
Hire or Buy? 42
Existing Services 44
Preparing the Site 45
Waste Disposal 46
Safety on Site 47

CHAPTER 4: GETTING STARTED 49

Drainage 49
Foul Water 51
Manholes 53
Rainwater Drainage 54

Drainage Connection 56
Drainage Trenches 57
Lintels Over Drainage Pipes 57
Safety 58

CHAPTER 5: GROUNDWORKS 60

Excavations 60
Underpinning 62
Setting Out 63
Foundations 66
Strip, Trench-Fill and Raft Foundations 68
Pouring Concrete Foundations 69
Below-Ground Masonry 70
Damp-Proof Course 71

CHAPTER 6: WALLS AND LINTELS 73

Starting Work 74
Removing the Garage Door 76
Cavity Wall Construction 77
Mortar 78
Cavity Wall Insulation 80
Wall Ties 80
Weep Vents 81
Indents and Profiles 81
Wall Plate 82
Party Walls 82
Lintels and Rolled Steel Joists (RSJs) 84
Bricklaying 86
Scaffolding 87
Scaffold Hire 88

CHAPTER 7: DOOR AND WINDOW FRAMES 89

Unglazed Window Frames 90
Window Templates 90
Thermal Bridging 92
Vertical DPC 93
Door Frames 93

CHAPTER 8: FLOORING 95

Upgrading the Existing Floor 96
Installing a New Floor 97
Preparing the Oversite 97
Concrete Floor Insulation 98

Contents

Damp-Proof Membrane 99
Underfloor Ventilation 100
Airbricks 102
Layering the Oversite Concrete 102
Levels 104
Beam and Block Floors 104
A Floating Floor 105
Floor Screed 106
Underfloor Heating 106

CHAPTER 9: TIMBER FLOORING 112

Suspended Timber Floors 112
Setting Out the New Floor Joists 114
Herringbone Struts/Noggins 114
Double Joists 115
Cables and Pipes 115
Floor Covering 116
Floor Insulation 116
Garage Roof Space 117

CHAPTER 10: ROOFING 119

Choice 1: The Flat Roof 120
Flat Roof Construction 121
Condensation 122
Cross-Ventilation 122
Setting Out the Flat-Roof Joists 124
The 'Firring' Section 124
Decking 124
Tilt Fillet 125
Felt Roofing 125
Choice 2: The Pitched or Sloping Roof 127
Pitched Roof Construction 127
Setting Out the Ceiling Joists 128
Lean-To Roof 130
Close-Coupled Roof 130
Hipped Roof 131
Roof Valleys 131
Gable Ladder 132
Fascia, Soffit and Bargeboards 132
Felt and Batten 133
Roof Tiles 133
Roof Slates 134
Cross-Ventilation 134
Cavity Tray 135
Lead Flashing 135
Guttering 136
Carpentry 136
Getting Quotations 137

CHAPTER 11: FIRST FIX 139

Internal Load-Bearing Walls 139
Internal Non-Load-Bearing Walls 139
Studwork Walls 140
Loft Hatch 142
External Doors 142
Made-to-Measure Windows 143
Glazing 143
The Glazier 144
Double Glazing 144
Door Linings 144
First Fix: Electrics 145
First Fix: Plumbing 146
Ceiling Boards 147
Fire Resistance 147
Loft Insulation 147
Second Fix: Electrics 148
Second Fix: Plumbing 148

CHAPTER 12: FINISHING OFF 149

Plastering and Skimming 150
Artexing 150
Dry Lining 151
Floor Tiling 151
Drying Out 151
Internal Doors 152
Skirting Boards and Architraves 153
Wall Tiling 153
Painting and Decorating 154
Tidying Up 155

ADDRESS BOOK OF TRADESMEN 156

USEFUL ADDRESSES 157

IMPORTANT CONTACTS 158

INDEX 159

Among the many homeowners trying to cope with today's ever-increasing demand for more living space there is a growing number who have found that converting their garage supplied them with both the easiest and the cheapest solution.

Of course this is not a 'one size fits all' solution, there are some areas where a garage can be an extremely valuable asset: garages in areas where parking 'off road' is extremely limited, where front gardens are almost non-existent and where secure vehicle storage is a necessity add to the saleability of a house. In these areas any other use of this space would be questionable. But in the vast majority of areas around the country the reality is quite different. Today we use our cars far too often to put them 'away' and, even if we were that diligent, garages were originally built for small cars, not the people carriers and four-wheel drive monsters currently frequenting our roads. Then add to this equation the steep rise in house prices in recent years. Moving is becoming more and more expensive, and moving to a larger property also carries a premium, so extending and converting will rank highly on every list of options.

It is for these reasons that the garage is now seen to be an area that has become far too expensive to continue as a storeroom. It is a veritable 'secret place' where bicycles, running machines, chest freezers and workbenches gather dust. It is a dry, weatherproof area where plans of fitness regimes and the production of do-it-yourself furniture were once nurtured with intensity but, in reality, were never destined to be seen through to the bitter end. Now the garage is rapidly loosing its identity within its original format, with more and more of them being included in the 'living' space agenda.

All of these are 'plus' points, and yet there are still more. An existing garage is already a built structure, often attached to the side of the house or as an integral addition to the front elevation. The walls, floor, foundations and roof are complete, making a conversion within the original structure simple and straightforward. The location, usually at the side of the house, will make it ideal to be included as a kitchen extension, a new dining room, or even a self-contained 'annexe' for use by an elderly relative requiring independent access, for example. For such an area the possibilities for improvement are almost endless.

Garage Conversions has been written as a fully illustrated, step-by-step guide designed to help you through this process. Starting with the initial survey looking at the suitability of your garage as a conversion, and continuing through to the endless range of possible layouts and uses, I think you will find this book invaluable at a time when you are making these important decisions.

> **'POINTS OF GOOD BUILDING PRACTICE' TO BE OBSERVED DURING CONSTRUCTION**
> During the building construction process there are many areas where shoddy workmanship and poor attention to detail can result in damaged materials, structural weakness and shoddy finishing.
> Through this book a number of these 'points of good building practice' have been selected to ensure that only the highest possible standards are maintained before and during the construction process.

Introduction

Every year plans are prepared by home-owners for them to change the use of the traditional garage to an extension of living space.

Whatever the reason for these alteration works, *Garage Conversions* has been produced to help throughout the initial design stages and through the entire construction process to completion.

Technically the new plans will require building regulations approval and structurally the possibilities may be limited, though it is always advisable first to check with your local authority before you make firm decisions. With the structure already in place, planning permission may not be required, though there is the possibility that the previous owner has exceeded the 'permitted' development allowance. Whatever the legal requirements a conversion will inevitably alter the elevations and appearance of your house with even the garden and driveway requiring alteration, so planning and design will play a vital role in the success of this increasingly common project.

As an addition *Garage Conversions* has included a number of 'points of good building practice' to be observed during construction. These points have been selected to ensure that only the highest possible standards are maintained before and during the construction process.

Garage Conversions has been written as a fully illustrated, step-by-step guide designed to help you through this process. Starting with the initial survey of your garage, looking at its suitability as a conversion, and continuing through to the endless range of possible layouts and uses, I am confident you will find this book invaluable at a time when you are making these important decisions.

MAKING PLANS

Adding, extending, improving, updating, remodelling and converting properties has of late become the norm, almost to the exclusion of all other activities. In fact, what was once an activity singularly driven by a buoyant and flourishing home housing market, this very British export, occupation and pastime has become ever more popular, even in areas not previously noted for their extensive building activity. For some time the huge number of ageing properties requiring improvement seemed infinite and the drive to bring them in line with the requirements of the twentieth and twenty-first centuries fuelled the flames, but then as the demand grew and the number of properties with potential decreased, the boundaries were raised. Popularized, in many cases, by the plethora of television programmes highlighting the benefits to be gained by the experienced and even novice builder (whatever the condition or location), it now seems that no country within the European Union has escaped the headlong drive toward improvement. This cannot be a bad thing in itself but the demand shows no immediate signs of abating, and while the demand for land and property is so intense, the true value of the range of property improvements available may be being masked.

Falling neatly within this and many other schemes is the conversion of an existing garage, barn or outbuilding. These are projects often within set parameters and also often within an existing design. That is not to say that it would be far easier and less expensive if the existing structure were to be razed to the ground and a completely new structure erected in its place, but this would hardly constitute a conversion (though the principals remain the same).

As with any building project, however large or small, its success or failure will lie in the planning. Planning should cover all aspects of the work from start to completion. Decisions must be made and finalized and advice, when required, must be sought. Expensive mistakes and costly errors lie in wait for the unprepared and inexperienced.

To start with, the viability of a conversion should be addressed. What space is available to be converted? What will be best achieved by a conversion? How much will it cost? And will it have the desired effect? This may be a DIY project, or if the work is complicated it may require extensive use of qualified subcontractors. With such a wide range of decisions to be made, making plans, and where possible sticking to them, is often the key to complete success.

In reality the reason for the conversion work may have nothing to do with property values and could be simply to accommodate a growing family, or perhaps to provide an annexe for an elderly relative, or to add to the existing living area. Whatever the reason, the work should be carried out to complement the existing property while remaining within the requirements that are laid down by local planning and building requirements.

Making plans

SITE SURVEY

Before any money is spent and any firm decisions are made it is important to size up the garage for suitability. Not all garages will work well with being converted and could after all prove to be a total waste of time and money.

Perhaps the plan will be to work within the existing structure and therefore limit the number of structural alterations. Alternatively, the plan may be to make the maximum possible use of the space available and even build above the garage. Whatever the considerations, whatever the hopes and plans, it would be wise, initially, to carry out a simple site survey to determine all the possibilities.

Of course, this initial and indeed crucial part of the planning process should be carried out by an architect or someone with similar expertise well before any firm plans are prepared, and be also used to determine any building control department requirements that must be addressed. The problem with this approach, if there is a problem, is that improvement and conversion works are likely to be led and controlled by the nature and shape of the existing structure, thus limiting the range of possibilities. Of course, the very first considerations must be given to what you would like to achieve by converting. Will you be able to end up with exactly what you want and will the existing structure satisfy or be moulded to meet your requirements? By starting from this position the project can be led by the hoped-for end result and not by the starting position.

Where possible, of course, it would be wise to familiarize yourself with a few of the more important building requirements. These can include points that may mean the conversion cannot be viable, or points that may push both the building and financial boundaries too far. These very important considerations will include: floor levels; drainage positions; ceiling or roof levels; and roof structure. If you find that these issues can be easily dealt with, then I am sure any sensible requirements planned within the structure can be achieved. It is at this stage, after you have decided loosely what you want to get out of the conversion, that an architect or draughtsman should be approached with a view to feasibility discussions and then eventually, hopefully, the preparation of building plans.

The architect will first consider the list of very important points that must be confirmed to ensure the viability of the project, such as floor levels and so on, and then, assuming these points can be satisfied, the design and structure of the new addition will be looked at.

High on the list, and this will seem fairly obvious, will be how the garage door is going to be replaced and whether or not the proposals will blend in with the existing property. Similar garages around the area may already have been converted, so ideas can be gleaned from the experience of others. Where this is not the case you will have to decide what you want to achieve from the front and also the rear elevation. The plan may be to replace the garage door with a large window. Alternatively it may be replaced with an entrance door or doors. The important point of the construction work required here is the position of the lintel over the existing garage door. Where this lintel is already horizontally in line with other lintels on the property the possibilities are improved, and where this is the case then adding a window or door should be straightforward. If the lintel over the garage door is higher or lower than other lintels on the property, then some work on raising, lowering or even replacing the lintel may well be required and will need to be considered.

Making plans

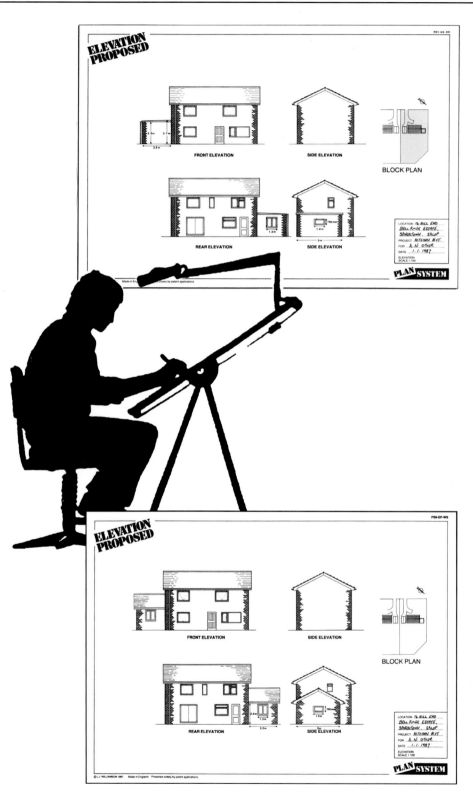

PLANNING PERMISSION

For a Planning Permission application, you will be required to submit plans showing the following:

- the existing elevations;
- the proposed elevations;
- the proposed floor layout;
- a block plan showing the new work in conjunction with the existing dwelling;
- an area plan showing the property and neighbouring properties.

BUILDING REGULATIONS

For a Building Regulations application, you will be required to submit plans showing the following:

- the existing elevations;
- the proposed elevations;
- the proposed floor layout;
- a section plan showing the construction details and structural design;
- a block plan showing the new work in conjunction with the existing dwelling;
- an area plan showing the property and neighbouring properties.

of the mains drain can often be close to if not through the garage area and relocation may be required. This does not necessarily mean huge additional expense; that will depend upon the depth of the pipes and, if drainage alterations are expected to be included in the plans, whether enough 'fall' can be achieved when the new pipework is installed.

Where this process becomes too complicated and a number of obstructions seem to thwart the original plan, then calling in a professional may well be the best solution. Contact the architect or draughtsman you want to prepare the final plans and arrange a meeting on site, where your requirements can be discussed in full.

A second important factor to take into consideration will be the existing floor levels. It is quite normal for the level of the garage floor to be lower than the existing house floor level, though simply raising this level may not be the answer. Headroom in habitable rooms is an important building regulations requirement and how it is achieved within this environment may not be clear-cut. Within the garage there may be structural beams, rolled steel joists (RSJs) and roof trusses set at a height that will determine the floor levels. Where this is the case and where it may be too costly to bring the garage floor level up to the existing house floor level, this may have to be sacrificed.

The third survey point is the roof. Is the existing roof structure to be retained or replaced? If it is to be retained then the timbers will need to be checked for suitability and this will be done when plans are prepared. You can check the roof timbers for rot or rainwater damage or any other visible damage that may require more serious action to be taken.

Finally, the location of services may well affect significantly what can and cannot be converted easily. The position

Building close to the boundary will bring a whole range of rules and regulations into play.

13

Making plans

PLANNING AHEAD

When the decision has been made about what the conversion is for and the proposed extent of the work, the next consideration is whether or not this new work requires the approval of the local authority. There are often clear parameters within which the developer must remain and there are boundaries around the property that must be adhered to. If there is any uncertainty about what is and is not permissible, then the best place to start will be the local planning office.

Before incurring the expense of drafting professional building plans, take a sketch of your proposals, showing clearly all the existing and immediate neighbouring properties, and discuss your plans with your designated officer. You may find that planning permission is not required and the work falls within permissible development – then only building regulation requirements need to be met. On the other hand, there may be any number of reasons why planning approval is required. These will include the amount of existing development already on the site, other extensions and so on, whether the building may be the subject of a listed building or preservation order, and the position of the building line may also need to be taken into consideration. Whatever the reason, full plans will need to be submitted either to the planning officer or a full planning committee.

A clue to any requirements may actually lie within the area you live. With the vast majority of houses and bungalows having been built in estate locations the likelihood of someone within the area carrying out a similar project will be extremely high. If you do live in such a location take the opportunity to wander round and see what others have done. If you do find a conversion similar to the one you are planning, call in and ask the owner if they would mind showing you the completed work. Ask them to explain the benefits and the pitfalls and glean from them the reaction they received from the local authority. It is likely they will extol the virtues of their new addition wondering how on earth they managed without it but listen for the 'buts' as well. Perhaps the door would work better elsewhere; perhaps the new window should have been larger. Try to gain from the experience of others.

During this decision-making process it is also important that you do not lose sight of what effect, if any, the new building work will have on your neighbours. It may be that the conversion in itself will not be a problem, but the amount of work involved – the noise, the mess and the regular delivery of building materials – could put a strain on even the closest relationship. So try to involve your neighbours from the very beginning. Show them your plans and try to prepare them for any potential inconvenience to come. It is important at this point to remember that where planning permission is required, the local authority will consult the neighbours for their appraisal

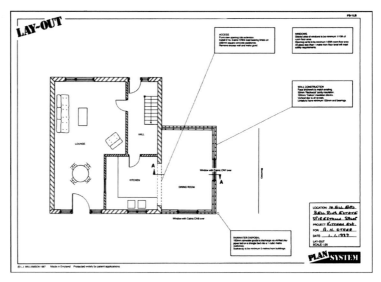

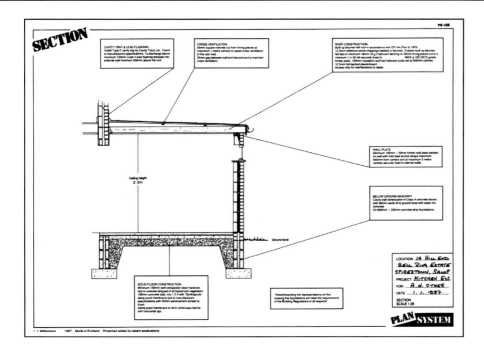

of the proposed works, so early approval will be an excellent starting point.

PLANNING PERMISSION

Converting an existing garage or out-building is not the same as a new extension because there is already a building in place, but the work may still need the approval of the local authority Planning Department. The existing building may only be a temporary structure and therefore may not have been included on the plans when the original planning approval was given. If this is the case then the requirement for planning permission may exist. If the building is a listed building then this is another reason why plans to convert should be discussed with the local planning officer before anything firm is decided. Where the building is of listed status then the amount of work it is possible to carry out without altering the protected status could be limited. For these and many other reasons it is important to find out as early as possible whether your proposals are, or are not, in line with local development plans.

Making plans

The Local Development Plan will be available at your Planning Department and it will outline all the aspects of the planning and environmental policies that the council has adopted and how they intend to carry them out. It is important at this stage to remember that the local authority Planning Department provides an invaluable service to the local community. In particular it is charged with preventing excessive over-development, or what is commonly known as 'urban sprawl', while protecting Green Belt areas and retaining the balance and character of the area as a whole.

Many garage conversions will not require planning permission. Under local permitted development rules, conversions and extensions of a certain volume and in specific positions can be built requiring only approval in line with building regulations. However, this also means that it is possible to build an unsympathetic and poorly designed conversion that can seriously affect the value of your property, create problems with your neighbours and alter the general appearance of the area as a whole. Sadly, these occurrences are not unusual and reinforce the need to discuss proposals with the local planning officer before firm plans are made.

Where a planning application is required, the Planning Department will provide the necessary forms and tell you how many need to be completed, the plans required and the appropriate fees. If the conversion is likely to be either extensive or controversial, then it may be wise to recruit the services of a professional. The quality of the application and the details shown on the plans may swing things in your favour if the decision is close. On the other hand, if keeping costs down is a priority when the likelihood of approval is slim, then perhaps sketch outlines will suffice in order to test the water.

When it is clear the proposals will meet with the satisfaction of the planning officer or the Planning Committee, then detailed drawings will be required. These should show the full extent of the new work and include front, rear and side elevations showing what effect the new work will have on the existing building, plus an overhead view (block plan) showing the immediate area around the building and an area plan showing the effect on properties in the immediate vicinity. Planning permission is not a set of rules to be ignored or flouted and planning officers can demand the removal of a building not meeting their criterion, so it is imperative to ensure that the correct approval is obtained before any building work commences.

Of course, not all conversions will require planning permission and there is also a scheme in place called the 'Permitted Development' scheme. This latter scheme takes into consideration the extent of building already carried out on the site. Where this 'permitted' figure is exceeded, or if this new work is likely to exceed it, then planning permission will be required automatically. Again, further discussion with the planning officer will help to determine any action to take.

Outline Planning Application

Unlike newbuild work, houses and extensions, conversion work cannot be the subject of an outline planning application. From the outset full detailed drawings will be required so it is important that professionals are used and that they are fully aware of what this space is to be used for.

LISTED BUILDING CONSENT

It is unlikely a listed building will have an attached garage, though unsympathetic alterations and additions may have been carried out before the building was officially 'listed'. Where such a garage exists it is unlikely to meet with opposition from the Planning Department providing the conversion work brings the building back to its original design.

As well as planning permission this work will require Listed Building Consent. This is a separate application and approval, required by the council, and it is likely that more detailed drawings showing the present building and the proposed alterations will be required.

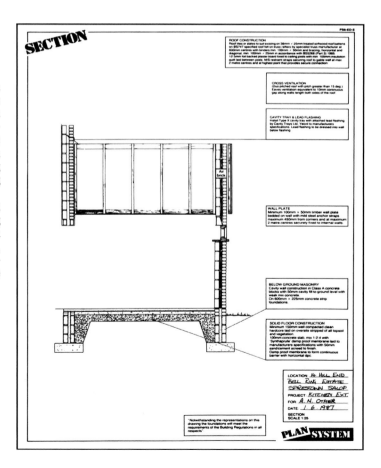

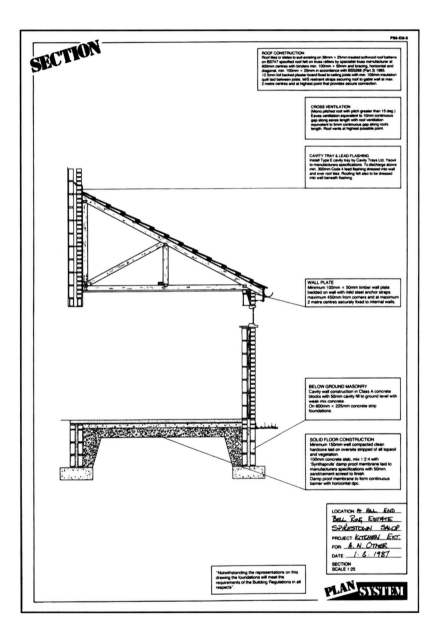

SECTION

P96-EM-5

ROOF CONSTRUCTION
Roof tiles or slates to suit existing on 38mm × 25mm treated softwood roof battens on BS747 specified roof felt on truss rafters by specialist truss manufacturer at 600mm centres with binders min. 100mm × 50mm and bracing, horizontal and diagonal, min. 100mm × 25mm in accordance with BS5268 (Part 3) 1985. 12.5mm foil backed plaster board fixed to ceiling joists with min. 100mm insulation quilt laid between joists. M/S restraint straps securing roof to gable wall at max. 2 metre centres and at highest point that provides secure connection.

CROSS VENTILATION
(Mono pitched roof with pitch greater than 15 deg.) Eaves ventilation equivalent to 10mm continuous gap along eaves length with roof ventilation equivalent to 5mm continuous gap along roofs length. Roof vents at highest possible point.

CAVITY TRAY & LEAD FLASHING
Install Type E cavity tray by Cavity Trays Ltd. Yeovil to manufacturers specifications. To discharge above min. 300mm Code 4 lead flashing dressed into wall and over roof tiles. Roofing felt also to be dressed into wall beneath flashing.

WALL PLATE
Minimum 100mm × 50mm timber wall plate bedded on wall with mild steel anchor straps maximum 450mm from corners and at maximum 2 metre centres securely fixed to internal walls.

BELOW GROUND MASONRY
Cavity wall construction in Class A concrete blocks with 50mm cavity fill to ground level with weak mix concrete. On 600mm × 225mm concrete strip foundations.

SOLID FLOOR CONSTRUCTION
Minimum 150mm well compacted clean hardcore laid on oversite stripped of all topsoil and vegetation. 100mm concrete slab, mix 1:2:4 with 'Synthaprufe' damp proof membrane laid to manufacturers specifications with 50mm sand/cement screed to finish. Damp proof membrane to form continuous barrier with horizontal dpc.

LOCATION: 14 HILL END BELL RING ESTATE SPIKESTOWN SALOP
PROJECT: KITCHEN EXT.
FOR: A. N. OTHER
DATE: 1.6.1987
SECTION
SCALE 1:25

"Notwithstanding the representations on this drawing the foundations will meet the requirements of the Building Regulations in all respects".

PLAN SYSTEM

INTEGRAL GARAGE

With building land in such short supply the larger developers are inclined to utilize every possible space and thereby greatly reduce the possibility of further enlargement, improvement or extension. In the drive to achieve the maximum number of dwellings on a building plot, designers search every avenue to save space.

One popular method of space-saving is the inclusion of an integral garage. This is where the garage is located within the main structure of the building. By doing this the 'footprint' of the building, the amount of land the building occupies, is space-sensitive. This will allow the developer the opportunity to build a room above the garage without altering the size of the building or the amount of land required. For conversion purposes a situation where the garage is integral to the building represents possibly the easiest of conversion projects. Unfortunately the amount of room available to convert is likely to be limited to the size of the existing garage and where additions and extensions extending beyond the building line are desired they will almost certainly need detailed plans and planning permission may be required.

LINK-ATTACHED GARAGE

A link-attached garage also offers conversion possibilities but boundary considerations will play an important part in any proposed conversion work. A design common to modern estate-built homes, the link-attached garage works well in principal but does not easily lend itself to conversion or extension. The problems inherent with building on or against the boundary line should, of course, be discussed with your neighbour to avoid future problems and plans showing how the party wall or any dividing structures are to separate the properties are best agreed before plans are drawn up. Building above a link-attached garage may also be a possibility, though the existing garage walls will almost certainly need upgrading to meet building regulation requirements. As with any conversion or extension work the requirement of planning permission will depend on both the individual merits of the work involved and how the local authority views the work when compared with the Local Development Plan.

DETACHED GARAGE

Where the garage is completely detached from the main property, discussions with the planning officer will determine what would and would not be accepted. A detached garage may be classed as an individual property, unless situated extremely close to the existing building, and is unlikely to be converted to be part of the main property in isolation. Extension works may be required to bridge the gap between the two properties. On the other hand this separation may well be the main attraction to conversion, allowing it to be used as an annexe to the main property where perhaps an elderly relative or relatives can stay, or even a student: close enough to be part of the family yet far enough away to retain independence. This type of conversion may, however, be fraught with obstacles from the planning officers. The further away it is from the main building the more likely the planning officers may treat the conversion in the same way that a new building would be treated. The proximity to the main building will be vital and there may well be restrictions placed upon how much development is allowed. Planning officers are often well aware how precedents can be set, so look around the area to see if anyone else has carried out a similar construction that can be used as a guide.

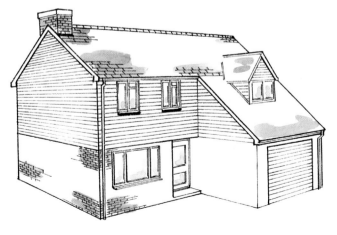

Making plans

In view of the huge variety of possibilities available when considering a garage conversion, including single-storey and two-storey conversions, it is difficult to provide a general rule on which decisions would ultimately be based. However, you can be confident in the fact that each project will be decided on its own individual merits and what effect the work will finally have on both the existing building and the buildings within the immediate area.

NO CHANGE

It is inevitable that converting the garage will alter the front elevation of the building; replacing a garage door with a window or wall, removing the driveway and adding an area of garden will make a difference. And it may be that such a course of action will not have the right effect on the building or the surrounding buildings. It is quite conceivable that such a dramatic change could produce quite the wrong result.

Where this is the case and the existing appearance (with the garage door and driveway in place) is best, then there are ways in which the conversion

work can go ahead and the garage door can remain in place. A typical example would be to build a wall inside the garage, some four or six feet back from the garage door, and to use this new area for the storage of garden implements, bicycles and so on, and build the new conversion behind the new wall.

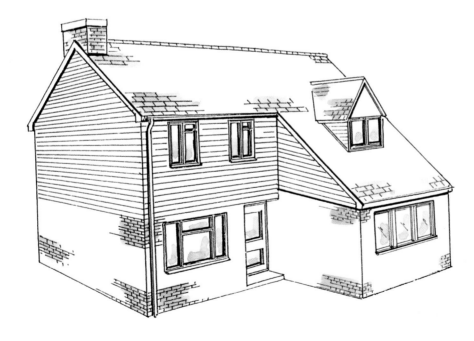

BUILDING REGULATIONS

Whether your new conversion does or does not require planning permission, it will require building regulations approval. Building regulations are rules approved by Parliament and laid down to ensure that the minimum design and construction standards are achieved in domestic and commercial buildings. The Regulations are a list of requirements, referred to as Schedule 1, that are designed to ensure the health and safety of people in and around the building, including adequate access and facilities for the disabled and the elderly and, very importantly, provisions for energy conservation.

Also included in the list of works requiring building regulations approval are alterations and additions to the drainage system; additions to washing and sanitary facilities; and construction work which alters the use of a building or is likely to have implications on adjacent properties – for example, work on party walls and underpinning.

To make an application for a building regulations approval there are three possible options to be considered.

Standard Application

The first and indeed the most common application for conversion and extension work is a full plans application. This involves detailed plans, clearly showing all the proposed building works and all associated constructional details. When the plans are completed they will be submitted to the local authority Building Control Department for inspection. When the plans are submitted the Building Inspector will check them to ensure that the design of the proposed structure meets all the requirements of building regulations. If it does not then the plans will fail and the areas in question will be listed so that they can be redesigned or upgraded. When the plans are approved an approval notice will be given, then the work will be inspected when in progress to ensure that it meets with the terms agreed on the plans.

Speedier Application

The second type of application is a building notice. With a building notice application plans are not required, though all sections of the work will need to be inspected by the building inspector as it progresses. This will greatly reduce waiting time (in terms of the approval of plans) but the work must comply in all respects with building regulations. This type of application can be used where time is short and where the contractor is fully up to speed with building regulation requirements, or it may be more suitable for small conversions and minor alterations than for any of the range of more extensive improvements.

Specialized Application

A third possible option is the use of an approved inspector. An approved inspector will check the building plans, oversee the building work and then, when the work is completed to the satisfaction of the inspector, an approval certificate will be issued. If the work is not completed to the satisfaction of the inspector, and it is important to remember that this applies to all other applications as well, an approval will not be issued. When this happens the inspector will be obliged to inform the local authority so that they can then consider the powers of enforcement available to them.

Whichever application you choose there will be a fee or fees required. A scale showing the amount to be paid, applicable to the size and value of the project, will be available at the planning office. A full plans application will involve two payments; a plan fee when the plans are submitted and an inspection fee due after the first inspection. For a building notice only one fee will be payable; it will be the equivalent of the full plans application and will be payable at the time the notice is given. Full details of the fee structures, all subject to VAT, can be obtained from your local authority Building Control Department. If you choose to employ an approved inspector, then the fee to be paid is a matter of arrangement between you and the inspector (this fee is also subject to VAT).

For the majority of garage conversions detailed plans will be extremely helpful during the construction process and will prove invaluable, initially, when obtaining quotations from builders and subcontractors. For these reasons a full plans application is recommended.

STRUCTURAL SURVEY

The extent of the work required to improve, upgrade and convert existing buildings may not immediately be obvious and will only become clear after a thorough survey of the property is carried out. Armed with an outline of the proposed building work the surveyor will calculate the suitability of the existing structure and also determine what is required to achieve building regulations standards. The depth of existing foundations, the strength of the walls, the floor and the roof will all fall within the requirements of a survey.

Of course, recruiting a surveyor will not be required in all instances. Where the conversion work is straightforward a competent DIY'er will be able to work with the Building Control officer to ensure the structure is built upon secure foundations and is structurally sound. The majority of attached garages are built initially with single brick walls and not the cavity walls required for living accommodation. For this reason, in some cases, the foundations required at the time of build may not have been to the same depth as the original house or to the same width. To see if this is the case the foundation will need to be exposed so that the building inspector can be satisfied that it is suitable for the new proposals. Similarly, the floor, walls, roof and so on will have to show whether they meet with approval or need to be replaced or upgraded.

Where there is doubt about the suitability of the existing structure the Building Control officer may request professional approval in the form of structural calculations. These can be obtained from the architect or from a structural engineer.

Work on party walls must be discussed in detail and the agreed to by the neighbours. In some instances written agreement may be required before any work can commence.

BOUNDARY

Making plans

STEP-BY-STEP SUMMARY

1. Before deciding to convert the existing garage space make sure the removal of this facility is not overtly detrimental to the property as a whole.
2. Look carefully at the effect of a conversion on the existing property and neighbouring properties.
3. Carry out a limited survey to consider the possible extent of work required and what limitations may exist.
4. Check with the local authority Planning Department about the requirement of planning permission.
5. Where extensive structural work is planned organize a survey of the existing property, to be carried out by the architect or draughtsman, to determine the extent of upgrading required.
6. Where the garage is situated close to or along the boundary line discuss plans with your neighbour to allay fears and encourage approval.
7. Of course your plans may not be original; it is always a good idea to check in the local area to see if similar work has been carried and what effect it has had on both the property and its function.

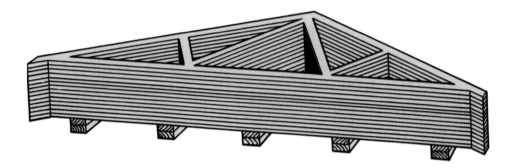

Stacking trusses.

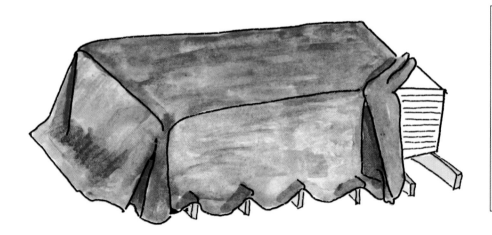

> **POINT OF GOOD BUILDING PRACTICE 1**
> All building materials must be protected from the elements. Where materials can only be stored outside they must be covered with suitable waterproof sheeting and the time exposed kept to an absolute minimum. Roof trusses and timber must be stacked off the ground and on a secure, level base.

INTERNAL PREPARATIONS

When planning permission and building regulation requirements have been determined, then the next step, almost inevitably, will be to get your architect or draughtsman to prepare detailed drawings for submission to the local authority for approval. It is possible, even with very little experience, to draw building plans of a suitable standard to be accepted by the council but often the structural requirements of a building regulations application can prove daunting. For this reason it is advisable, in order both to maximize the potential of the property and to capitalize on the experience of qualified professionals, to recruit an architect or draughtsman to prepare the building plans. Using professionals at this stage can add confidence to the application that may well work in your favour. Of course, choosing between an architect and a draughtsman may not

accurate quotation of the fee must be obtained before you give the go-ahead for plans to be prepared. If changes are made to the original plans, then there are likely to be extra costs involved. Always check at each stage what is and is not included in the fee. There will also be a fee payable to the local authority (cheques should be made out to the Local Authority and not the architect) when the plans are submitted and, on top of this, there may be additional costs if structural calculations are required. An outline of the costs involved may be given on first contact, over the telephone, and then determined after a site visit.

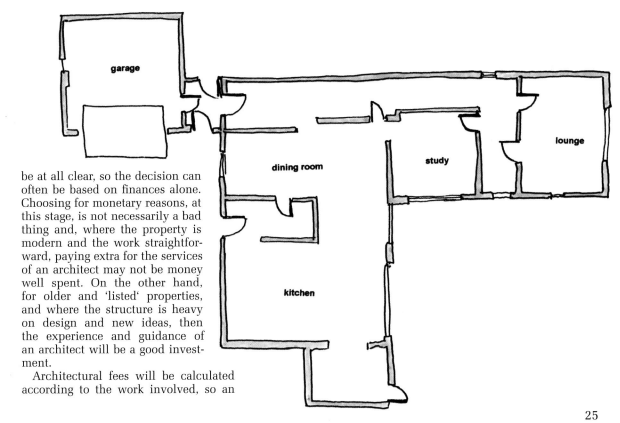

be at all clear, so the decision can often be based on finances alone. Choosing for monetary reasons, at this stage, is not necessarily a bad thing and, where the property is modern and the work straightforward, paying extra for the services of an architect may not be money well spent. On the other hand, for older and 'listed' properties, and where the structure is heavy on design and new ideas, then the experience and guidance of an architect will be a good investment.

Architectural fees will be calculated according to the work involved, so an

Internal Preparations

When the plans are completed and submitted to the Local Authority for approval, then quotations can be obtained from contractors for all or part of the work. It is important, at this stage, to remember that the plans may not be approved as they stand and changes may need to be made. This can cause confusion when the contractor quotes for one thing and is then expected to build something quite different. For this reason it is often best to wait until the plans are passed before approaching tradesmen and contractors for quotes.

PREPARING A FLOW CHART

It is at this stage of the project that the size of it and time frame involved in carrying it out becomes more important. When the local authority approval is given it is quite normal for the work to be expected to start within a limited time period. When planning permission is granted and the work is not started within the stated time a fresh application may be required.

There are also other, similarly important factors to be considered. These include obtaining quotations from tradesmen, arranging materials deliveries and setting out storage areas. For this reason keeping an accurate diary or flow chart showing each stage of the work, the date of deliveries, and the arrival and completion of the different trades is important. The accuracy of the flow chart will depend upon good planning, and the art of good planning is confidence. If you feel confident that this whole project is merely an opportunity to progress and succeed, rather than a problem to be solved, then the whole experience will be both beneficial and rewarding.

How this record of future events is kept will be left to the individual. Perhaps a computer spreadsheet showing predicted times, dates and deliveries accompanied by another spreadsheet showing what actually happened would be a good option. For some a diary is best and others will use a flow chart designed just for this project. Whatever is used it must be kept up to date and the information included must be accurate.

Before any or all of this information can be collated effectively, quotations from suppliers and tradesmen will be required. This need not be a chicken-and-egg situation. It is likely that the materials required will be readily available, often within a day or two, whereas the tradesman could well be booked up for some months in advance. So, unless the materials required are unusual and non-standard (such as matching bricks and roof slates, handmade windows and so on) it will be best to approach the trades first so that their time can be scheduled before material deliveries are requested.

ADDITIONAL PLANS

The flow chart you prepare will show how the building work is expected to progress. It will simply be a diary of planned events showing how and when materials will arrive and what date tradesmen are expected to start and finish their particular section of the work. To accompany the flow chart, there will inevitably need to be other plans around which the success of the project will also be determined; plans not prepared by the architect but necessary for the tradesmen to work from.

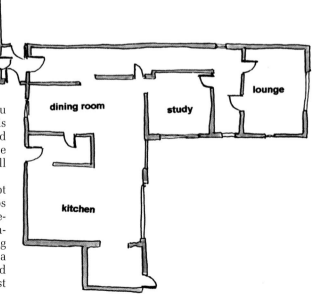

'Yes madam. We ask for half before we start, then the other half when the work is completed.' 'Of course we do accept cash!'

Internal Preparations

Of course the most important set of plans will be those prepared by the architect and from which the new structure will be built. These plans will include any new drainage, because drainage is subject to building regulations, but they may not include the other services such as gas, electricity and central heating. Where these are absent an additional sketch plan should be prepared showing what is expected: additional radiators to be added to the existing system and their location; electrical power points and light fittings, including how many and where. All these will depend on what the new conversion is to become. It may be an annexe requiring kitchen facilities or it may simply be an additional reception room, or a dining room, where these services are not so important. Other plans, less important but necessary for the smooth running of the project, will include a plan showing any materials to be reused (and those to be discarded), a garden plan and a material storage plan.

Contractors and tradesmen will need sight of all these plans to ensure that their work does not impinge on any of them. Undoing work can be expensive and throw the whole process into disarray.

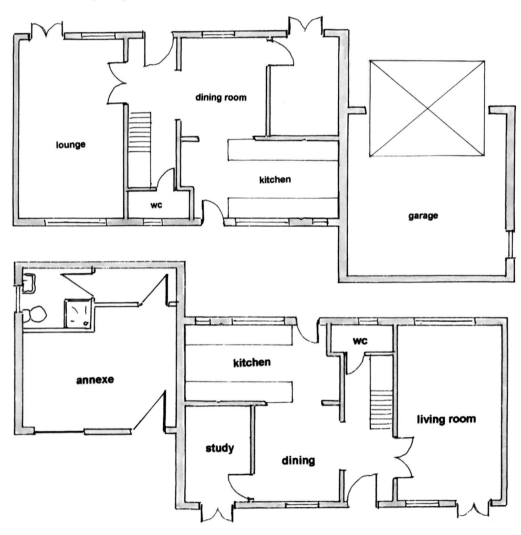

OBTAINING QUOTATIONS (TRADESMEN)

For the best possible results and to ensure the smooth running of your project, use the best tradesmen you can find. Quality may cost just a little more but its value is timeless and will repay you time and time again in quiet satisfaction.

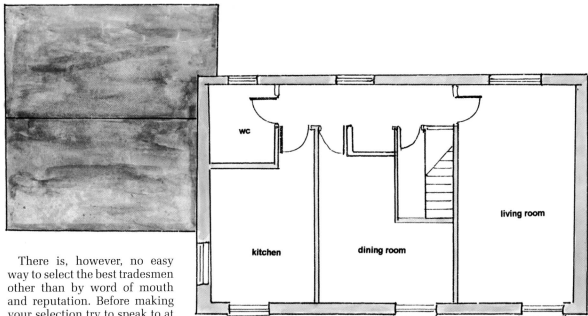

There is, however, no easy way to select the best tradesmen other than by word of mouth and reputation. Before making your selection try to speak to at least a couple of previous customers and, if you feel it necessary, ask your Building Control Department. It is unlikely they will go so far as to recommend an individual tradesman or company but they may be able to help you with your selection and, importantly, steer you away from any unscrupulous operators lurking in the shadows.

After selecting the trades to quote for the project, make sure each has a clear view of the plans and, where possible, visits the site. For smaller projects, a site visit may not be necessary as there may be very little to see, but if, for example, the area to be converted is very confined and close to the boundary, then a site visit to see the extent of any problems would be wise.

Internal Preparations

The quotations should be given in writing to avoid any dispute and should clearly outline all the work included in the price. There are three clear categories for pricing work within the trade and all are designed to ensure fair play to both parties. The first and most popular is a fixed-price agreement where the tradesman agrees to complete a certain project for an agreed fee. This is an excellent method but relies upon both parties understanding clearly what is and is not included in the price. Where doubts arise after a quotation is given, be sure to ask as many questions as necessary so that there are as few 'grey' areas as possible. All too often the homeowner feels ripped off because the final bill bears no resemblance to the original quote. In the majority of cases this is based on a misunderstanding of exactly what was or was not included in the quote.

The second method is based on the amount of work involved, or a 'metreage' price. This method will be more applicable to plasterers and bricklayers where they work on a certain rate per metre of wall or per thousand bricks.

Of course, in many cases the full extent of the work involved may not be all that clear. Demolitions and excavations fall neatly into this category and tradesmen or contractors may well hold back from giving a firm quotation for this type of work. Where this is the case the third, and in many cases, more risky method of 'day rate' is used. To say this method is risky does not mean it is unfair or slanted toward the contractor and away from the customer: far from it. This is a very fair way of getting work done to the satisfaction of both parties. There is, however, an element of risk, in that close control of the work and a higher-than-usual level of honesty is often required to avoid large overpayments.

When the quotations are all in, the selection process may be on price alone or on other factors. There is a realm of thought that says you must accept the lowest price, but this is not always the case with smaller domestic projects where the emphasis is more likely to be on appearance and attitude, with the contract often going to the most suitable applicant.

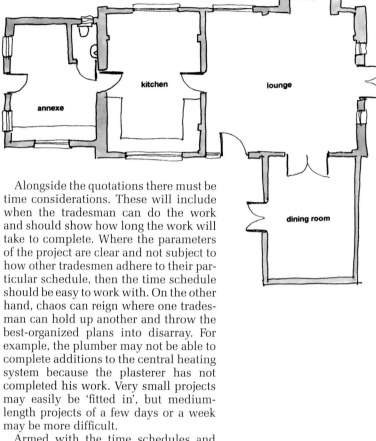

Alongside the quotations there must be time considerations. These will include when the tradesman can do the work and should show how long the work will take to complete. Where the parameters of the project are clear and not subject to how other tradesmen adhere to their particular schedule, then the time schedule should be easy to work with. On the other hand, chaos can reign where one tradesman can hold up another and throw the best-organized plans into disarray. For example, the plumber may not be able to complete additions to the central heating system because the plasterer has not completed his work. Very small projects may easily be 'fitted in', but medium-length projects of a few days or a week may be more difficult.

Armed with the time schedules and availability, the spreadsheet or flow chart can be updated and arrangements made for material deliveries.

OBTAINING QUOTATIONS (MATERIALS)

After the plans have been approved and quotations obtained from tradesmen, it is then time to organize materials. Depending upon the size of the project and the space available, materials will probably need to be ordered and delivered in phases. Where storage is limited, a closer eye on deliveries will be important to avoid delays and disappointment should a tradesman arrive to start work only to find that all the materials necessary to complete work are not available, causing delay and disruption.

To get quotes for building materials, it is a good idea to approach at least two local builders' merchants for prices. Where possible, open a trade account and negotiate the best discount possible. If the project is substantial the builders' merchant may price for supplying all the materials 'off plan'. To do this they will work from the approved drawings and quote for supplying all the materials. A good overall discount may be negotiated where this is the case.

VALUE ADDED TAX (VAT)

When calculating the total build costs the inclusion of value added tax (VAT) cannot be avoided. This is an additional non-reclaimable cost to the project and can be significant. Material suppliers will be required by law to charge VAT for the goods they supply and this will be added, if not shown, on their invoices. The inclusion of VAT in prices at the outset may not be all that clear, so it will be important to ask whether or not VAT is included in any prices you are given.

Paying VAT to builders, contractors and subcontractors may be quite a different story. In the main, medium-sized builders, depending on the building company's annual turnover, will be required to charge VAT for their work and will be required to specify this clearly in their quotation. Where this is the case they must show, on the quotation, a current VAT reference number. This reference number must also be shown clearly on any invoice for work completed.

Unfortunately, this taxation can be used and abused by the less scrupulous contractor, who could potentially charge VAT when not registered and see it as a way to make additional profit from the work. If you are not sure how authentic the contractor is, you can contact your local Customs and Excise office for advice. Adding VAT when it is not necessary can quickly increase the costs of a project, often without questions being asked.

Smaller builders and tradesmen are less likely to be VAT registered so exercise a degree of caution here when a request for VAT is made. Again, check with the local Customs and Excise office if you are at all unsure.

Spotting the 'cowboy' builder is not as easy as you may think.

FINDING A BUILDER

Smaller domestic building projects will generally be best served when a good quality local builder is employed to carry out the work. Of course, some money can be saved by employing individual contractors to carry out their specific trades but the organization of such an exercise can reach nightmare proportions and is often best left to the professionals. Finding a good local builder, however, may not be as easy as it sounds and the media is constantly filled with stories to sharpen the mind.

When trying to find this golden nugget in what may appear to be a sea of problems there are certain guidelines to observe and rules to enforce. Finding a good builder will be the end of the story. Managing your builder to carry out the work within the agreed time and the agreed budget will involve some skill and a great deal of man management. Builders, you will find, are (on the whole) a very honest and helpful bunch. They want to please and they want to complete the project in the agreed time so that they can then move on to the next project. A good builder will always have a next project.

The first place to look for your established builder will be the *Yellow Pages*. The fact that a builder advertises in the *Yellow Pages* does not automatically mean he is a good builder. The reason for looking will be to identify the builders within close proximity for consideration. Draw up a shortlist. Builders specializing in smaller building projects will often be able to offer a more competitive price and be able to recruit tradesmen who are used to working on smaller building projects.

From this shortlist select three or four for further consideration. There is no hard-and-fast rule about this: if there were, life would be easy, but there is not. Some building companies will be newly formed and others may have been established for years; neither point is a sign of a good or less good builder. Using three builders selected from your final shortlist, the following process is one that I feel will work in your favour and give you confidence in your selection.

Contact all three builders. Tell them of your plans and that you want to invite

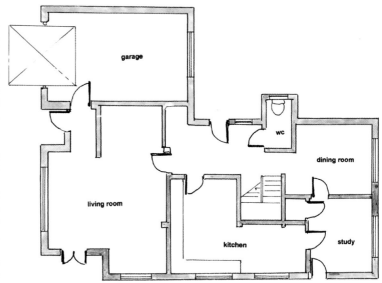

them to tender for your work. If they are happy with this, then ask if you can meet them, on site, on their current building project. This course of action may appear to be out of sequence but it will give you a first-class opportunity to see the 'ship they run' and to help you decide whether or not you would be happy with them carrying out your work. If you like what you see, invite the builder to visit you at home with a view to quoting for your work. If, when you contact the builder, he does not have a current project to visit, I suggest you either wait until he has one or you select another builder. Make sure of course that each builder quotes from the same set of drawings and for the same work.

When you have selected the builder of your choice, you can seek references if you wish. Sadly, this area of references can be flawed. I suggest you revisit the project with which you are already familiar and speak to the owner. This way you can have first-hand, up-to-date knowledge of the builder's current work.

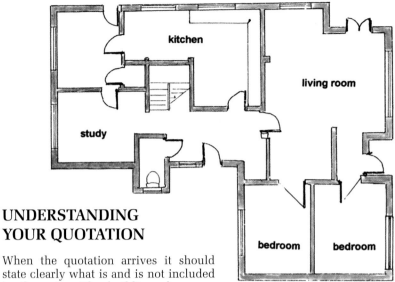

UNDERSTANDING YOUR QUOTATION

When the quotation arrives it should state clearly what is and is not included in the price. The building plans you provided will form a major part of this contract. If there are any grey areas the quotation should clearly state this. If the builder feels that there is some part of the work he is unable to price accurately, such as underpinning the foundations for example, it is quite acceptable for a 'provisional' sum to be included in the quotation. If this section of the work is more difficult than anticipated, then there may be an additional cost after the provisional sum has run out. A provisional sum is not a ploy used by the builder to get more money. It is a safeguard to protect the builder and his business where certain aspects of the project may be just too difficult to price accurately.

Where there are items for which the purchase will be decided at a later date (perhaps a bathroom suite, a new kitchen or a staircase), then the builder may include a 'prime cost' sum. This is a fixed sum set aside for the purchase of that item. If the item exceeds that sum then there will be the difference to pay; if it is less than the sum, then that will be taken off the final bill.

Provisional sums and prime costs sums are there to protect the builder and the customer. Leaving these to chance may result in the builder allowing for only a basic item whereas the customer had in mind something a little more 'classy'.

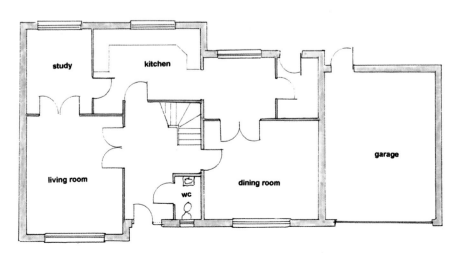

PAYMENTS

The old adage 'money talks' is as true in the construction industry as it is in any other walk of life. However, extra caution must be taken before handing over large sums of money in this business. A building project may well be the

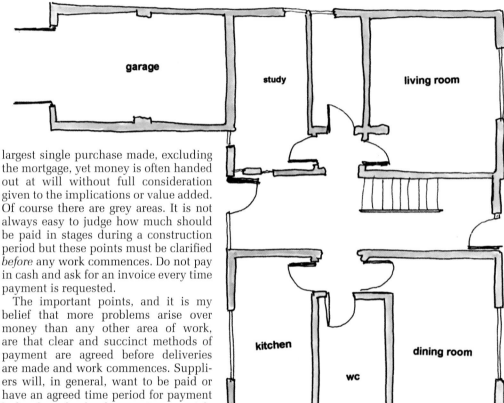

largest single purchase made, excluding the mortgage, yet money is often handed out at will without full consideration given to the implications or value added. Of course there are grey areas. It is not always easy to judge how much should be paid in stages during a construction period but these points must be clarified *before* any work commences. Do not pay in cash and ask for an invoice every time payment is requested.

The important points, and it is my belief that more problems arise over money than any other area of work, are that clear and succinct methods of payment are agreed before deliveries are made and work commences. Suppliers will, in general, want to be paid or have an agreed time period for payment before lorry loads of expensive materials are delivered. Some will expect payment before the delivery is made, others will accept cash on delivery (COD), and some will agree to a monthly account. Whichever method you use be sure to pay only for the materials supplied and check every delivery to ensure you get exactly what you pay for. Do not accept shoddy or damaged goods and ensure you return or have replaced anything you are not happy with.

Paying tradesmen will require more care, and making payments before work is carried out must be avoided at all costs. In special circumstances a tradesman may ask for payment or a deposit towards expensive or special items. This

is not unusual, nor is it unreasonable, though it should be specified in the quotation. Payment or deposits for any other reason should be treated with a great deal of caution. There are two significant guides for making payments to tradesmen and these, you will find, support standard practice.

The first, and most common with private and domestic building works, is when the tradesman expects to complete the work within one week, for example. It may then be agreed that a single payment will be paid on satisfactory completion of the work. When this is the agreement, then the money should be available, on time, as agreed.

STAGE PAYMENTS
Do not pay for work that has not been carried out. Staged payments should be an amount owing for completed work and can be calculated at any stage. Never pay for work not carried out and always retain a sensible final payment to be paid on completion.

The second method of payment, also common with private and domestic projects, is where the work will exceed one week and may run into several weeks. Of course, it is unreasonable to expect the tradesman or men to work for long periods without payment, so a method of payment will need to be agreed. This method of payment is likely to be based on the work completed at the end of each stage. Knowing how much to pay is often difficult to assess and must be dependent upon how much work has been completed and how much work is then left. Try not to overpay in the initial stages because work seems to be going at a pace. This can leave little or no incentive for the contractors to complete the remaining work, especially where there is little or no money remaining.

What is not standard practice and should be strongly advised against is payment for 'labour' before the work in question is completed or even started. Of course, not all tradesmen – in fact surprisingly few – are unscrupulous and overcharge but being forewarned is forearmed. It is well known that there is practically no area in life where we can avoid being duped but I am confident that, if you follow these simple rules, pitfalls will be avoided. I am also confident that you will find the vast majority of skilled tradesmen put their reputation long before financial gain and on completion of the project you will number several new names in your list of friends.

ORDERING MATERIALS

A significant part of the planning and the success of any construction project, however large or small, will be the availability of both labour and materials. One cannot operate in isolation from the other. For this reason the art of managing incoming materials, and it is an art, may well determine the overall smooth running of your project. Where room for storage is plentiful and there is also good, dry storage for the materials that require protection from the weather, then deliveries can be received several days or even weeks before they are required. Some of the more delicate materials, which include cement powder and

plaster, are considered to be best when they are fresh and therefore will benefit from being delivered just prior to use. Even where this is the case and storage is only very temporary it will need to be suitable, ensuring the materials can be used when required.

Of course the real art of managing materials can be seen when storage space is at a premium. A common sight is that of building materials piled high in and around front gardens with heaps of sand and ballast often spilling over onto the pavement or highway. In these instances and where good, dry storage is very limited good planning is essential in order to eliminate problems, reduce waste, reduce the risk of theft and, very importantly, reduce the stress placed upon neighbours.

Where space is at a premium the deliveries will need to be well organized and storage, even when very limited, must be adequate to prevent not only weather damage but also the likelihood of theft. The cost of materials stolen from building sites every year is staggering, with the further unseen cost often being paid in the form of delays to the building work itself.

When planning the overall storage package try to ensure that all materials are quickly stored away, distributed

around the site to where they will be required and, when exposed to the elements, protected as much as possible against bad weather.

'Who is running this site?' 'I keep running out of materials.'

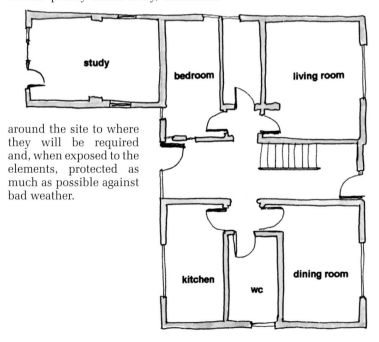

SAFETY AND INSURANCE

On-site safety is paramount for the occupants, for visitors and for contractors, with the emphasis on the developer to ensure that public liability insurance/site insurance is in place to protect all participants. Of course, every possible precaution should be made as far as protection is concerned. Scaffolding will be erected with handrails, and hard hats provided for visitors to the site, but there will be other members of the public for whom protective insurance is a must. These will not only include the house occupants but visitors such as the postman and milkman. The tradesmen themselves are likely to have their own insurance and protective clothing but on site unexpected and unusual circumstances do arise and this insurance will at least provide the necessary personal and financial protection.

RISK ASSESSMENTS

The requirement for risk assessments to be carried out before and during the construction process will depend on the number of workers working on site at any particular time. If you are the main contractor responsible for hiring in subcontracted labour and for the overall site management, then the responsibility for carrying out risk assessments is yours. Where there is a main contractor, a builder for example, and it is their responsibility both to hire in subcontracted labour and deal with the overall running of the building site, then the responsibility for carrying out risk assessments is theirs. At the time of writing, where the number of workers at any one time exceeds five, then a daily risk assessment is required and diary notes should be made.

It may be obvious to you that the area is hazardous but do not take this for granted. Barriers should be erected around holes and obstacles and clear signs must be in full view. Other typical areas to assess will include open trenches and scaffolding. Make sure that excavations should be covered when not in use. Ladders should be properly secured, both top and bottom, and it should be ensured that scaffolding and scaffolding planks are not removed for use somewhere else on site, or the structure tampered with. For example, a tradesman may require a plank to stand on temporarily and may remove one from the scaffolding but forget to return it when the work is complete. This type of 'borrowing' will leave areas of extreme danger for anyone walking on the scaffolding.

To make sure you do not fall foul of the insurance company's rules and regulations regarding site insurance, check with them about when you will be required to carry out risk assessments and what risk assessment notes they require. Any literature they can provide to help during the construction period will be very helpful. Of course builders, contractors and tradesmen will be required to have their own insurance but they will still have the right to sue anyone responsible for the site should accidents occur due to the negligence of others.

Site safety must take a high priority. Insurance is a 'must'.

STEP-BY-STEP SUMMARY

1. Select an architect or draughtsman to prepare the detailed drawings for application to the local authority for approval.
2. When approval is received discuss your plans with skilled tradesmen and get quotations for the work.
3. Break down the plans into material requirements and get quotations from builders' merchants.
4. Prepare a spreadsheet or flow chart showing material delivery times and the available dates of the key tradesmen.
5. If you are using a local builder make sure you follow the appraisal procedure before getting quotes.
6. Get quotations from at least three builders.
7. Go through the complete project with them to ensure you both understand fully what is required.
8. Make sure public liability/site insurance is in place.
9. Carry out a risk assessment on the site every day while workmen are there.

> **POINT OF GOOD BUILDING PRACTICE 2**
> Window and door frames must be built into walls using the appropriate fixings for the purpose. Nails in wooden frames are not appropriate.

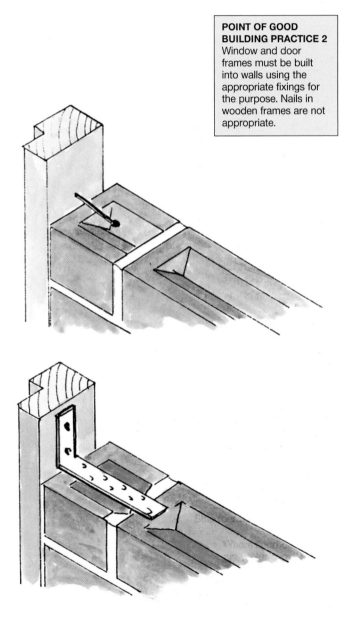

EXTERNAL PREPARATIONS

When all the necessary paperwork is in place, proper consideration can be given to the practical elements of beginning the project. For this there is no 'one size fits all' rule. In fact, to convert any existing building, there will almost certainly be provisions linked to the building regulations approval. True, the plans prepared by the architect will comply, as they must, with building regulations, or they will not be approved. On the ground, however, the detail may well be completely different. Take the foundations as a prime example. When the garage was built, there is unlikely to have been a requirement in place to ensure that the foundations will be suitable for a building other than a garage, unless the garage is an integral garage. The depth, width and indeed the thickness of the concrete used for the foundation may be totally inadequate for any new plans. This may be obvious from the outset or it may require further investigation to find out fully the extent of upgrading required. Similarly, the garage floor, also installed for the purpose of being just a garage floor and likely to be set at a significantly lower level than the house floor, will need investigation so that full provision can be made to improve it to meet the new requirements.

In many restoration cases the complete removal of the existing building and a rebuild from scratch will be both the cheapest and the quickest option. Where this is the case and the garage is to be removed and completely rebuilt or replaced in its entirety, then plans for storage of the materials to be reused and for the disposal of all unwanted waste will be required. Simple sketch plans along with instructions should be available during the discussion period with contractors so that everyone will be aware exactly what is to be salvaged and where incoming materials are to be stored. Do not leave it to chance: this can prove to be extremely costly and inconvenient. Recovering dumped materials or relocating a pile of sand to somewhere else on site can be time consuming and can create unnecessary tension.

Whether you are removing and rebuilding or simply filling in where a garage door once was, consideration will have to be given to any effect the work will have on your garden. Established trees and plants may need to be removed and relocated and the existing driveway, currently running into the garage, will need redesigning. The storage of materials, position of waste disposal bins and even where cars will be parked during the construction work will have an impact on the garden. For this reason the renovation and refurbishment cannot be treated in isolation.

STORING MATERIALS

The very fact that this is a garage conversion implies that space is at a premium and this will be made even more restrictive because of the need for parking spaces for vehicles. It may be that all the weather-sensitive materials can be stored inside the existing structure as the conversion work continues, and it may be that there is plenty of room for heaps of sand without affecting general access to the home. Where this is the case and there is plenty of room the building works and material storage all too often spread out around the site, eventually occupying far more room than necessary. On the other hand, where storage and access are at a premium, clever and

Make sure that all materials stored outside are protected against inclement weather conditions.

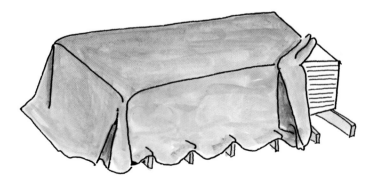

skilful storage will reduce the impact on site and ideally allow normal everyday life to proceed almost seamlessly.

Where materials are to be stored in the dry and there is enough space, then further protection may not be required; you need to concentrate only on the proper rotation of the materials as they are used and as new deliveries arrive. Keeping a close eye on each stage of the building work will ensure that the materials for each particular stage are handy and are not buried under materials to be used at a later stage of the construction.

Where the storage is outside, then exceptionally more care must be taken. Materials will include the more bulky items such as sand, bricks and blocks and these must be covered for protection against the weather using tarpaulins or similar protective sheets. It is important to remember that hot, dry weather can be almost as damaging as wet weather, particularly with sand. The sheets can be removed as required and then replaced when not in use.

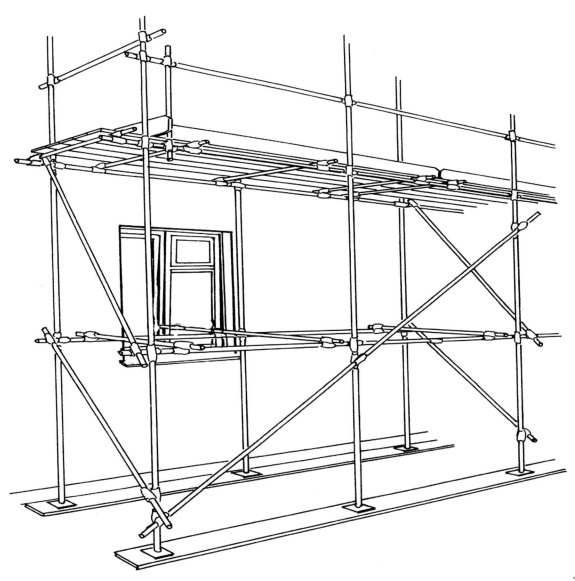

ROOM TO WORK

Converting any building will produce demands of space as with any building project, and the garage is no exception. By its very nature space will invariably be limited within the building as well as around it, so due consideration must be given to the room required for each trade to carry out the work involved. The balance between storage space and working space may be a very close call but room for the tradesmen to carry out their trade is primary and the greater the space they have, the happier they will be. For this reason an area around and within the building to be converted should be left completely free from hazards so that standard building practices can be pursued, such as the erection of scaffolding and the transport of materials from their storage to the point of use.

Make sure all the necessary approvals are in place before work commences. Good planning often leads to good results.

PLANT AND EQUIPMENT HIRE

An absolute boon to the smaller building contractor and invaluable to the DIY enthusiast, plant and equipment hire ensures both the availability and the affordability of the larger items of plant and machinery required to carry out building projects more speedily and professionally. There are three clearly defined methods of plant hire associated with the building and construction industry, of which two are common to home extension and conversion works and the third can sometimes be used with the larger building projects but is more common to sizeable developments.

The first is the hire of items to be used by the hirer or the tradesmen employed by the hirer. These items include cement mixers, tarpaulins, trestles, ladders and so on. The second is where the hired equipment is delivered and erected by specialist firms. This category will include scaffolding and waste disposal skips. The third, more common with larger development projects, includes items that are hired with an operative. This section includes JCB diggers with driver, and tipper lorries with driver.

Hiring in expensive plant and machinery to be used on minor works ensures that the costs involved can be kept to a minimum, allowing all types of building project to fall well within the remit of the keen DIY enthusiast. Add to this the competitiveness of the now thriving plant-hire business and it is clear that this can only be good news for the end user.

There is a word of extreme caution, however. Many of the items available for hire can be very dangerous, even deadly, in the wrong hands or when used without the proper protective equipment. Make sure each item of equipment hired is done so *with* the correct protective clothing, goggles and attachments. The plant hirer should ensure these items are available at the point of hire whether or not they are included in the price.

Storage conditions should be dry, safe and secure.

External Preparations

HIRE OR BUY?

Of course the contractors' equipment hire boon has been a revelation for the DIY industry as well but there are times when hiring may be a more costly decision than buying outright. Making this decision will inevitably involve larger upfront expenditure but the project must be looked at as a whole. Some of the tools required might be just too expensive and will not recoup the initial investment, and these should be hired; other less costly items or those used for longer periods may be another matter. In listing a few of the items of equipment required for home extension and conversion works, I have tried to be as cost effective as possible.

Excavation Works

This section of the construction process will require small tools such as shovels and pickaxes, and may even include a JCB, mini-digger, skip and compactor. Of course, it goes without saying that the purchase of a JCB for a garage conversion will be a slight overspend and that hiring such major plant as those listed here would always be the recommended option. But the smaller tools mentioned here, also including a wheelbarrow, sledgehammer, crowbar, hose-pipe and water butt will almost certainly be better to buy than hire.

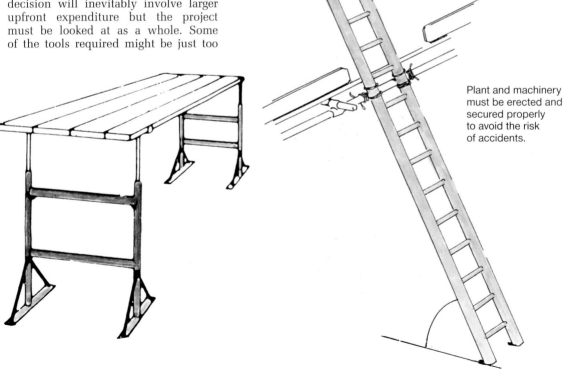

Plant and machinery must be erected and secured properly to avoid the risk of accidents.

Wall and Roof Construction

This section of the construction will require a similarly wide variety of tools. Smaller tools will include spirit levels, trestles, ladders and a cement mixer. Larger items may include scaffolding, planks, hoists and acrow props.

Due consideration must be given to each item in this section because trestles and acrow props do not really fall into the DIY category and may never be used again. Try to calculate the length of time for which these items will be required and consider how the sums add up. Trestles will almost certainly get more use than acrow props, and that will go for planks as well. There is a buoyant second-hand sales market for many similar tools and this avenue may provide many solutions.

Tools apart, there is a growing section of the hire market covering such items as tarpaulins and dust sheets. Take a good long look at everything you will require to complete the project in its entirety: look at what tools the contractors will provide, list the rest and look around for the best solution.

On the other hand, where the project is to be handed over to a builder he will have included these items in his cost-ings and no further payment should be required unless, of course, unexpected items arise during construction necessitating a review of his price. For example, if there is a clause in the builder's initial quotation covering the depth of foundations and then the building inspector demands a deeper foundation than specified, the builder may need to bring in plant to carry out this work and add this additional cost to the original quote.

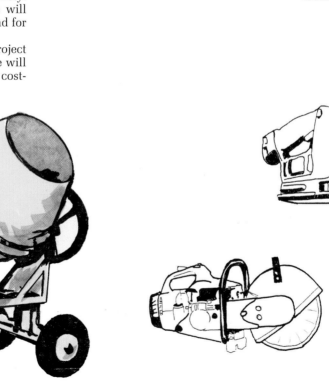

EXISTING SERVICES

Plans for substantial alterations, especially when they are outside the existing perimeter of the building, must take account of incoming services. For properties where gas, electricity and mains drainage are connected, then it is very likely that these services will all be situated close to the building, in some respect. This would be either as a direct connection leading straight to the building or buried around, often within very close proximity to the building itself. Needless to say, extra care must be taken where excavations are carried out. Where this is the case these services may need to be re-routed: building over services is not always the acceptable option so professional advice should be sought before decisions are made.

'Mains' drainage is a common building term for any waste water and sewage drainage connecting a property to either the main local drainage system or an individual system such as a sewage treatment plant or septic tank. The requirements of building regulations will be the same. When re-routing mains drainage or when the plan is to build over existing drains, building regulations will apply so permission must be sought (if it is not already approved on the building plans) from the local authority Building Control.

PREPARING THE SITE

From an early stage the area set aside where the work is to be carried out will have been designated in principle. Where the conversion work is within the existing building parameters, then the area concerned will need to be cleared of all obstacles and storage areas clearly defined. Where the work extends outside the existing building parameters, then site clearance will become a priority before work can start.

These obstacles may simply be plants and moveable obstructions including fencing or gates. More substantial obstacles requiring temporary removal may have been included in the contractor's agreement. Where the latter is the case, make sure it is fully understood with the contractor or tradesman who is expected to carry out this work. Delays and extra costs may well result where there is no clear agreement and the work starts on the wrong footing.

This will also apply to the delivery of incoming materials. For bulky materials including sand and bricks, clearly designated areas must be agreed and their location must be realistic. Delivery drivers will be limited to their areas of access and, even with modern crane-operated vehicles, cannot be expected to search out suitable areas of storage. Where you or your representative cannot be on site to receive deliveries, always leave sensible instructions for the driver designating storage areas well within reach. When the materials to be deliv-

ered may be vulnerable to damage in bad weather and undercover storage is not possible, protective sheets or tarpaulins must be available to provide protection after offloading.

Where excavation work is involved outside the line of the existing building, all visible obstructions such as paving slabs, plants and shrubs should be removed so that the precise area for this work can be marked out. Where obstructions are below the surface and their location is known, it may be wise to leave a clear indication of their location to reduce the risk of an incident. Using sand as a marker, the area to be excavated can be clearly marked.

The majority of garage conversions will not extend beyond the existing building line and the excavation works will usually include removal of the existing garage floor to be replaced with a fully insulated, waterproof replacement. Where this is the case the area will need to be cleared so that the work required can be carried out.

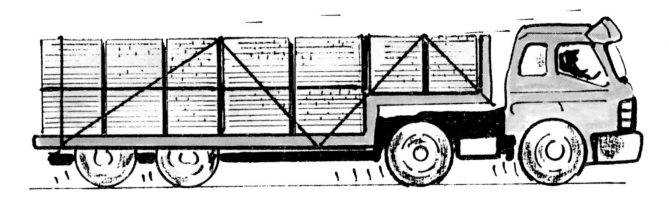

WASTE DISPOSAL

There is practically no area of the construction process where rubbish and waste materials will not be produced, often in abundance. A small proportion of the general building rubbish, bricks, blocks or concrete from the existing garage floor where it is removed may be used as ballast to assist drainage in the soakaways and may be suitable to back-fill where foundation trenches have been produced.

Before using any waste materials always check with the building inspector about their suitability for the purpose. Some bricks will not be suitable for use below ground as they degrade sufficiently over time to affect the building process.

Where excavations are carried out the topsoil can often be dispersed around the site or sold off to neighbours. But in the majority of cases the waste and rubbish – and this will include subsoil from the trenches and oversite excavations – should be removed from the site at regular intervals to reduce the risk of untidiness. Working in this way from the start of the building work will not only keep the site area tidy, it will also encourage tradesmen and workers to do likewise.

Disposal of building waste is proving to be a problem for local authorities. Fly tipping, a method used by the lazy and unscrupulous, is not acceptable and many areas now have clearly designated areas for waste disposal. If you are unsure about their location the council office should be contacted.

There are two common methods of removing waste materials from site. The first, and a very popular choice for small domestic building projects, is the use of waste disposal skips. Skip hire companies are well known and plentiful in all areas and this method of waste disposal is extremely popular, providing an excellent and competitive service. The skip or skips can be hired for an agreed period of time and the hire charge will include any tipping charges, delivery to the site and collection.

One waste disposal skip can hold a large quantity of waste and, with good timing and regular contact with the skip supplier, it can be replaced when it is full, often at short notice. Estimating how many skips will be required for the excavations may be tricky but a calculated guess should suffice. Soil increases in volume when dug so calculate the volume of any excavation trenches, multiply the total by one and a half times and this should give you an indication of the amount of soil to be removed and how many skips you are likely to require.

When ordering skips, and in particular skips where there is easy access by the general public, try to arrange for their delivery early on the morning you expect to start work, leaving as much time as possible to fill the skip and get it removed. Leaving a skip empty overnight may well attract the attention of locals wanting to dispose of their unwanted items such as old bicycles and old pieces of furniture, often under cover of darkness.

Hard hats must be available to be used on site at all times.

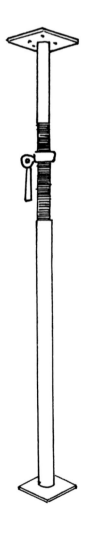

Before ordering a skip it is important to give consideration to where it is to be left. Where the hire is short term, a day or two, the position will not be so critical but with longer hire extra care should be taken. There may also be a limit on accessibility for delivering and removing the skip.

If the skip is to be left on the roadside, the public highway, the supplier must be given plenty of notice so that a licence can be obtained. If overnight hire is also required then lights must also be arranged. The skip hire company will deal with these items provided suitable time is given. Do not leave a skip overnight on the public highway without lights. Accidents do occur, often resulting in prosecutions. And finally, if it is not possible to fill the skip during the day be sure to cover it with a tarpaulin or similar sheeting overnight.

The second, and often popular, choice of waste disposal for smaller development projects is to hire a tipper lorry, with or without a driver. The waste soil and building rubbish can be disposed of at local tipping sites for a fee, and the lorry can also be used for collecting small quantities of sand, ballast or pre-mix concrete. With smaller building projects, ordering small quantities of such materials can come at a premium when they are delivered to site, and these delivery fees must be considered when making your calculations.

SAFETY ON SITE

Demolition and excavation works are sites where accidents are prevalent. Every year many thousands of injuries and a number of deaths occur on building sites around the country, and many are preventable. To ensure your building site is safe check regularly that open trenches and excavations have barriers around them and/or are covered with materials such as planks to prevent accidents. Do not cover trenches and holes with sheeting or tarpaulins that simply hide the obstruction.

It is the responsibility of the main contractor to ensure that all equipment, whether owned or hired in, is safeguarded against injury and that all the necessary protective clothing, including hard hats, gloves and goggles, are available on site should they be required.

SAFETY
Accidents, by their very nature, are difficult to avoid and building sites are noted accident black spots. To avoid adding to the statistics every precaution must be taken. Always keep the site free from hazards, keep it tidy and do not leave open excavations as traps for the unprepared. Plant and machinery should have warning signs and hard hats must be available at all times. Accidents do still happen, however, so make sure you have third-party and site insurance for the duration of the work.

Excavations must be covered and never left unattended.

External Preparations

Where equipment is hired, then it is the responsibility of the hire company to provide suitable protective clothing to be used with that particular piece of machinery. However, do not leave anything to chance. When hiring in plant and machinery always ask the supplier about protective clothing.

It is the responsibility of the subcontractor to ensure that proper shoes and clothing are worn for everyday site work.

STEP-BY-STEP SUMMARY

1. Check around the site to determine where materials will be stored ready for use.
2. Ensure work areas are not blocked off by materials or other obstructions.
3. Check which items of machinery will be hired in from plant hire specialists.
4. Make sure all contractors and tradesmen working on the site are familiar with the location of incoming services such as gas, water and electricity.
5. Ensure that all plants to be relocated after the construction work are set aside out of harm's way.
6. Ensure all contractors and tradesmen are familiar with all the materials to be saved from the demolitions, to be reused in the new building and that they are stored in a safe place.
7. Where waste disposal skips are to be sited on the highway, make sure the hire company has plenty of notice to obtain the necessary licences. They will not leave a skip on the highway without a licence. Delays can arise.
8. Where skips are located on a highway, overnight lights will be required to prevent accidents. The skip hire company will provide the necessary equipment.
9. Site safety must be given the highest priority. Never leave holes and trenches open and unattended and make sure unsafe areas where demolitions and building work are continuing are well guarded, and notices are provided.

POINT OF GOOD BUILDING PRACTICE 3
Packing under timber joists must be kept to a minimum and only rigid materials should be used.

GETTING STARTED

The building plans are approved and all quotations have been received. Everything possible to do in preparation has been done and now it is time to turn theory into practice. Where to start? Well, with completely new work the answer to this question will be a fairly easy one; with a conversion, however the answer to this question may well set the stage for the rest of the work.

It would be impossible for me to set out a strict work rotation or regime without having first sight of the approved building plans plus a site visit. Some of the work schedule will be fairly obvious but will also need to be carried out in conjunction with the overall plan.

The term 'site' has already been used and will be used again several times in this book so it is important to understand its meaning. First of all, there is the site in general. This is the area allotted to carry out the whole of the building works, including material storage, waste disposal and even car parking for the contractors. Then there is the building site in particular. This is the area, the precise location, where the actual work is to be carried out. The approved building plans will show the building site in particular, including all newbuild and renovation works. Plans for the building site in general should be available and should show where and how materials to be reused will be stored, where new materials are to be stored and where waste disposal skips are to be dropped off. When all these plans are prepared, then the physical work can commence in earnest.

DRAINAGE

Additions to the existing drainage system must have been calculated and added to the building plans submitted to the Local Authority for approval. Any additions, however small, to the existing drainage system will to subject to building regulations approval and will be inspected when installed.

It is in my view without doubt that the single most important factor in this country's health and well-being since the beginning of time is the invention and construction of our modern drainage system. To maintain the high standards that currently prevail, and in order to protect the general public from serious, sewage-related diseases, all new drains must be capable of carrying foul waste, without leakage or blockage. This process must be carried out in a manner that fully complies with current building regulations and this will apply ,whether foul waste discharges into local public sewers and drains, or into septic tanks and sewage treatment plants where public sewers are not available.

Adequate protection must be afforded to drainage pipes where they pass through walls and foundations.

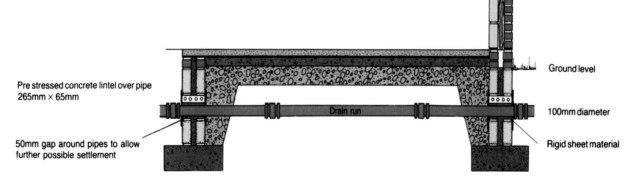

Pre stressed concrete lintel over pipe
265mm × 65mm

50mm gap around pipes to allow
further possible settlement

Ground level

Drain run

100mm diameter

Rigid sheet material

Installing a new W.C. and
inspection chamber.

FOUL WATER

The discharge from a lavatory basin (WC), hand basin, bath and kitchen sink is called 'foul water' discharge, whereas water discharged from roof guttering and land drainage gullies is called 'surface water'. The disposal of foul water from domestic premises will fit into one of two categories. The first method of disposal will be via the local authority mains drainage system. This system is common and is used in all urban and the great majority of rural areas. The foul water waste will discharge through a mains drainage system to the public sewer, where it will be treated in local authority sewage treatment plants. The second method of foul water disposal, where a mains drain connection is not possible, will be into a septic tank or sewage treatment plant. These individual plants will be emptied at intervals by professional operatives and the sludge waste will often be discharged onto local farmland.

Surface water (rainwater) is treated in a different way and will be disposed of via a mains surface water drainage system installed parallel, though not connected to, the mains drainage system, and it is discharged into canals and rivers. Where mains surface water drainage is not available, surface water can be dispersed on site into a soakaway.

Any additions to the existing foul water drainage system will be subject to building regulations approval before any work can start. The design and layout of the new additions should be kept as simple as possible with the minimum of bends and plenty of access points to deal with potential blockages.

It is important, and a prerequisite of building regulations, that new drains carrying foul water waste away from domestic dwellings into the public sewer system are installed correctly. They must be laid to the correct fall so that the discharge travels easily through the system and they must be leak-free. For this reason drain-laying is a skilled job and the approved building plans must be followed carefully.

The choice of drainage pipe will be either vitrified clay or plastic uPVC, of which the latter is becoming more and more common in domestic situations.

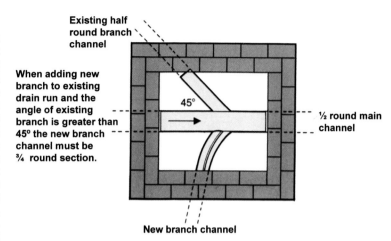

Existing half round branch channel

When adding new branch to existing drain run and the angle of existing branch is greater than 45° the new branch channel must be ¾ round section.

45°

½ round main channel

New branch channel

The pipes can be easily cut to size using a standard handsaw and the couplings are easy to fit. Whatever the type of pipe selected they will need to be securely bedded on a granular base (pea shingle is commonly used), laid evenly and not covered over until the building inspector has inspected them. The usual fall into the drainage system is 1 in 40. This can be more in some instances, so it is wise to follow the details on the approved building plans.

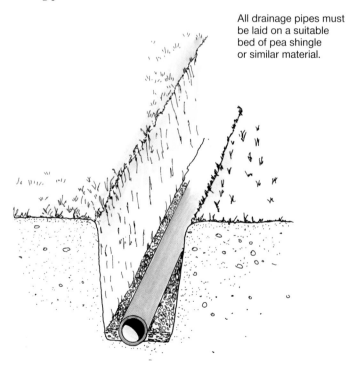

All drainage pipes must be laid on a suitable bed of pea shingle or similar material.

Getting Started

Where the drainage pipes are to pass through walls or under buildings, they will require adequate protection from damage. Where the pipes are close to or within 300 mm of the ground level they will need to be protected, perhaps covered in concrete, against damage by traffic.

To avoid destabilizing existing and new concrete foundations, drains passing within 1 m of the foundations and below foundation level must be encased in concrete up to, and at least level with, the base of the foundations.

Where the new drainage pipes pass through walls a lintel will be installed above the opening with a gap of at least 50 mm around the pipe to allow for any settlement. A rigid sheet can be fitted around the pipe, covering the open gap to prevent access by burrowing animals.

A major part of the installation process is the trench-digging. By allowing about 100 mm extra trench depth for the addition of the granular bedding base for the new pipes to be laid on, and 150 mm around the pipe in order to provide sufficient space for jointing and proper compaction of bedding materials, the result should be an even and secure system.

The gradients of the new pipes, as specified on your building plans, can be prepared by using a gradient board or a string line to confirm the pipes are laid to the correct fall. The granular bedding

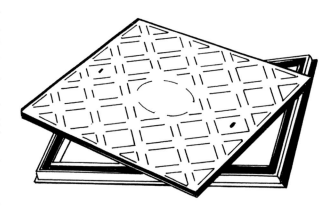

should be added, then the pipes laid on top of it, taking care to avoid breaks or cracks. The building inspector will inspect the new drains and may carry out a drain test to ensure the seals are secure and the risk of leakage is minimal.

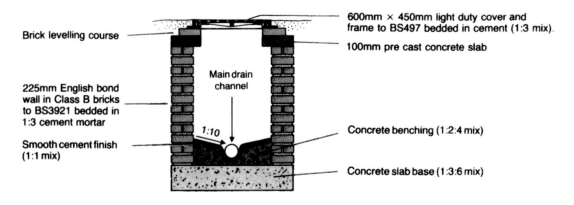

Brick levelling course

225mm English bond wall in Class B bricks to BS3921 bedded in 1:3 cement mortar

Smooth cement finish (1:1 mix)

Main drain channel

1:10

600mm × 450mm light duty cover and frame to BS497 bedded in cement (1:3 mix).

100mm pre cast concrete slab

Concrete benching (1:2:4 mix)

Concrete slab base (1:3:6 mix)

Brick inspection chamber.

MANHOLES

An inspection chamber, more commonly known as a manhole, serves two purposes. First, it provides a junction where several drains will meet and form one drain, and second it provides a point of access to the drains where rodding canes can be inserted to clear blockages should they occur.

Where inspection chambers are less than 1 m deep there will be a choice of materials you can use. Preformed polypropylene chambers are available in sections dependent upon the depth and are easy to install. Alternatively, the original style of manhole, brick-built off a concrete foundation, can be used. The walls should be 225 mm thick, built in English bond brickwork and constructed using semi-engineering bricks, suitable for this purpose because of their density.

In the base of the inspection chamber the channels meet and discharge their waste into the central main channel. Standard household drains are generally constructed from 100/110 mm diameter pipes, although larger sizes are available and must be used where specified. The side channels entering the inspection chamber to connect to the main channel must do so at an angle of less than 90 degrees, directing their waste along the main channel and with the flow of the drains.

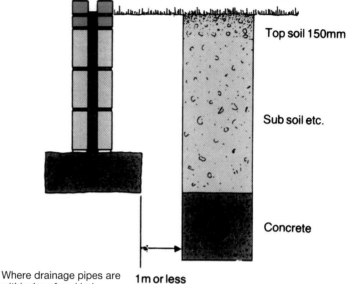

Top soil 150mm

Sub soil etc.

Concrete

Where drainage pipes are within 1m of and below the foundations they will be encased in 1:3:6 mix concrete level with the base of the foundations.

1 m or less

PIPE COVER LIMITS	Minimum covering
Fields and gardens (on 10mm granular bed)	300mm
Light traffic, driveways etc. (on 10mm granular bed)	400mm

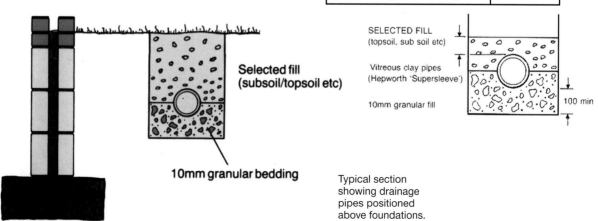

Selected fill (subsoil/topsoil etc)

10mm granular bedding

SELECTED FILL (topsoil, sub soil etc)

Vitreous clay pipes (Hepworth 'Supersleeve')

10mm granular fill

100 min

Typical section showing drainage pipes positioned above foundations.

Manhole Covers

The type of manhole cover required will be determined by the location of the manhole. There will be a wide range of covers from which to choose, all designed with a specific purpose in mind. If the manhole is in a position where it will be exposed to heavy traffic, including cars and suchlike, then the cover must be designed for and suitable for this purpose. Similarly, if the manhole is located in the garden and is unlikely to be subject to anything other than light foot traffic, then this cover will also need to be suitable for the purpose. Of course, heavy-duty covers can be used in any location whereas light-duty covers will have strict limitations.

Where the manhole is located within the building a double-sealed cover will be specified. This type of cover has been designed specially to prevent noxious gases and odours from entering the building whilst allowing access to the drains should blockages occur.

RAINWATER DRAINAGE

The rainwater discharged from roofs and other areas is classified as surface water and is either discharged into a public surface water drain or into a soakaway. Where the rainwater is discharged into a public drainage system it is quite likely that any additions can be connected to the existing system without recourse to upgrading the existing drainage system. Where the rainwater discharge is into a soakaway, then additions to this system may well require the provision of a completely new soakaway.

When a new soakaway is required it must be positioned to ensure that the disposal of this surface water and rainwater will not affect the integrity of any foundations or buildings within a 5m radius of the soakaway. If you have any doubts about the permeability of the ground where the soakaway is to be positioned or its ability to cope with this extra influx of water, discuss the problem with your building inspector who may be able to advise how soakaways operate within the designated area.

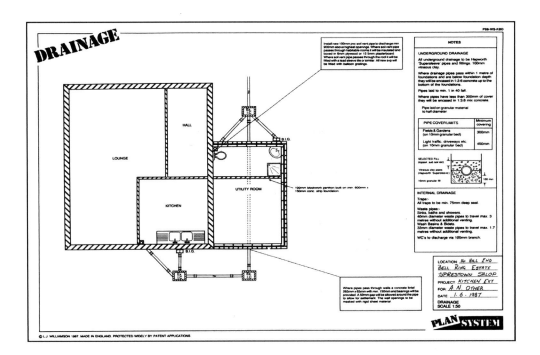

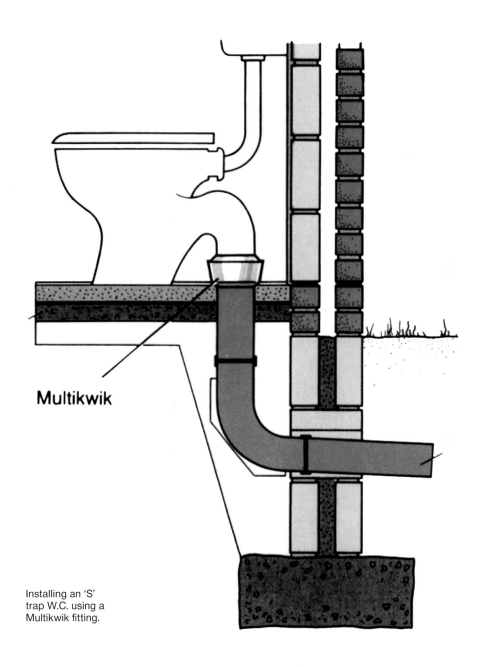

Multikwik

Installing an 'S'
trap W.C. using a
Multikwik fitting.

DRAINAGE CONNECTION

Where conversion works include the disposal of foul water into new or existing drains then approval will be required from Building Control. Where the addition is within easy reach of the existing drains the process should be uncomplicated and therefore designed to operate smoothly, without the risk of blockage. Where the addition is situated some distance from the existing drainage system, and where the new work changes direction, a series of points will be required where access to these junctions can be easily achieved for the purpose of reducing the risk of an inaccessible blockage. This emphasis on access and prevention will be required not only where the drains change direction but also where there is a long drainage run.

When the building plans are prepared and approved these access points may be shown as rodding eyes or inspection chambers. Building inspection chambers at every junction may appear excessive but access will be required at all junctions. An alternative is the use of rodding points as these can provide a very effective alternative to inspection chambers and they are often acceptable to Building Control. A rodding point, or eye, is a preformed section designed specifically for access to the drains to deal with blockages, should they occur.

The drainage connection for small conversions and extensions is likely to be a single connection and full details should be shown on the building plans. Where a toilet or bathroom is to be added a new inspection chamber, where the new drains join the existing drains, is likely to be required.

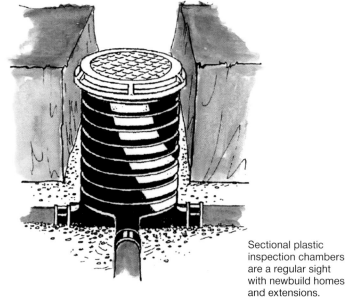

Sectional plastic inspection chambers are a regular sight with newbuild homes and extensions.

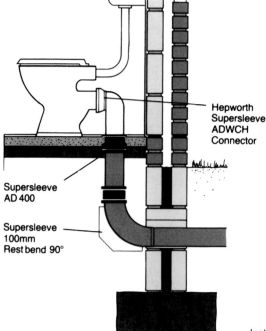

Hepworth
Supersleeve
ADWCH
Connector

Supersleeve
AD 400

Supersleeve
100mm
Rest bend 90°

Installing a new W.C. 'P' trap using a Hepworth Supersleeve 'ADWCH' connector.

Where the new work involves a kitchen and a kitchen sink or a wash-hand basin, then a back inlet gully will be required. Again, this should be specified on the building plans. There are several types of back inlet gully available, to suit every possible need, and they can be installed internally or externally as shown on the plans. A back inlet gully operates in the same way that a toilet 'trap' operates. A bend at the base of the gully is filled with water at all times and prevents noxious odours and gases being released from the gully or the building area. Where the back inlet gully is situated internally a screw-down lid will be fitted. This lid can then be removed, if required, to provide access should blockages occur.

DRAINAGE TRENCHES

Any new drainage trenches can be excavated at the same time as the footings or underpinning works are carried out, retaining the soil for covering the pipes after they are laid. Before the pipes are covered over they will need to be checked by the building inspector. The drainage trenches should be dug out, either mechanically or by hand, to a depth required to achieve the necessary fall on the drain run and to a width so that installation can be carried out successfully. The fall on the drain run will be specified on the building plans and is likely to be 1 in 40. This fall is required because the majority of drainage systems are gravity-fed. The foul waste will require this fall, or gradient, in order to discharge successfully.

When the drainage trenches are excavated an allowance of approximately 100mm in the depth must be included so that a layer of pea shingle can be laid beneath the pipes as a secure and level bed.

LINTELS OVER DRAINAGE PIPES

Where drainage pipes pass through the foundations and walls, lintels will be required to act as a suitable bridge over the pipes. Full details will be shown on the approved building plans; however,

below ground level pre-stressed concrete lintels are often found to be the best option. As with all lintels, an end bearing (that is, how much of the lintel is resting on the walls adjacent to the opening in the wall) of 150mm must be allowed. The surrounding walls will be built fairly tight to the drainage pipes but there will be small openings around the pipe where burrowing animals can dig under the extension. To avoid this, cut a rigid sheet to fit around the pipe and to cover over the hole in the wall. Secure this sheet in place before backfilling the foundation trenches.

Adding a section to existing drainage pipes.

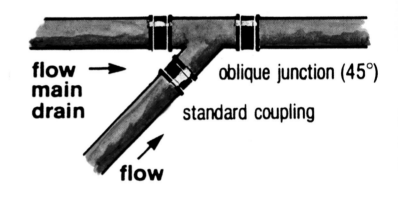

flow → main drain

oblique junction (45°)

standard coupling

flow

Providing rodding access to new drainage pipes.

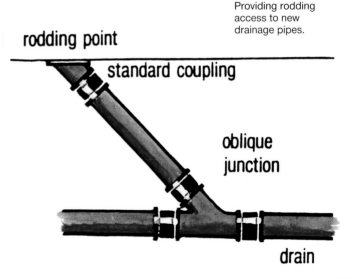

rodding point

standard coupling

oblique junction

drain

SAFETY

Where drainage or any other trenches are to be excavated extra precautions should be made in the way of safety. It is not advisable to leave trenches uncovered overnight because of the very high risk of accident or injury.

Any holes or trenches left unattended must be covered over or guarded. This will also apply where the ground conditions and prevailing weather conditions fill the excavations with surface or ground water. Where this is a possibility and where ground conditions become dangerous, be sure to fill in trenches at the earliest opportunity.

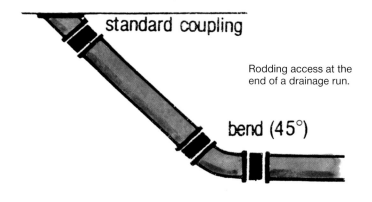

Rodding access at the end of a drainage run.

The location of incoming drainage pipes for WC connections must be precise.

STEP-BY-STEP SUMMARY

1. All drainage additions must be secure from leakage with easy access where the drains meet or change direction, to ensure that blockages can be dealt with easily. The building inspector may request a drain test to check for possible leakage and to prevent localized soil contamination.

2. Make sure the new drains are laid to the correct fall. A gradient board or a string line can be used to check the installation.

3. All new drains should be laid on a granular bed, such as pea shingle, and will be subject to inspection by the building inspector before they are covered over.

4. Inspection chamber (manhole) covers sited in areas where there is traffic, whether motorized or foot traffic, must be suitable for the purpose.

5. Where inspection chambers are sited inside buildings, double-sealed manhole covers will be required to prevent noxious odours and gases or waste materials entering the building.

6. For safety's sake make sure open trenches and soakaway holes are covered or guarded when left open overnight.

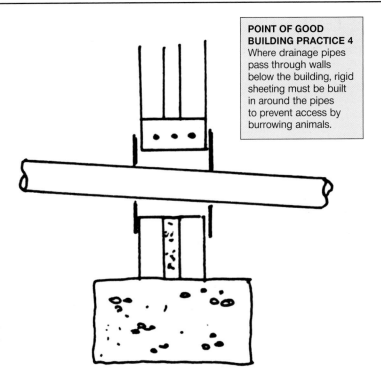

POINT OF GOOD BUILDING PRACTICE 4
Where drainage pipes pass through walls below the building, rigid sheeting must be built in around the pipes to prevent access by burrowing animals.

GROUNDWORKS

The full extent of the building works involved in a garage conversion may only be small in comparison with an extension or a newbuild but the principles will remain the same. The work must be carried out to the same exacting standard and must meet with all the required building regulations. In fact, smaller works such as those involved with conversions and renovations can be very taxing and often require a higher degree of ability than simply laying new work in new trenches. Any additions to the existing drainage or foundation system will have tolerances to work to and levels to follow. Where this is the case the existing drainage and foundation depths will set a precedent and it is from these levels that the architect will have calculated depths and falls.

EXCAVATIONS

When all the preparation work has been completed the excavation work can start. There are quite a few areas within the business of construction where there is a choice of how to carry out the work and excavation is one of them. With a standard garage conversion the excava-

tion work is likely to be along the lines of underpinning or upgrading existing foundations and putting in foundations for new internal walls. Where this is the case, and in particular where room to work is limited, there is usually only one appropriate method of carrying out the work and that is by hand.

Digging footings and working at or below ground level is really not ideal. This work is extremely strenuous and should come with a health warning to the uninitiated or unprepared. Recovering in hospital from a body breakdown can play havoc with the flow charts, so extreme caution is advised.

A new foundation may be required where a garage door is removed and a new wall is to be built.

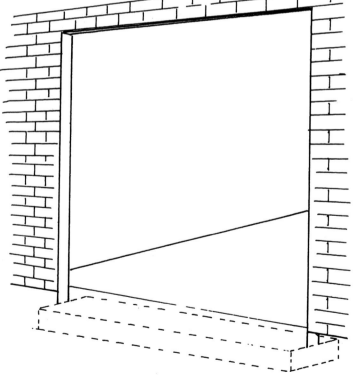

Apart from the health risks the process of digging by hand requires extreme caution because of unknown hidden dangers. Always make yourself aware of drainage pipes and incoming services such as gas and electricity before any work starts, even though their exact position may not be easy to determine.

For larger works, where the foundations are likely to be deep or where the existing building or large sections of it are to be newbuild, then a mechanical digger may be the best option. Where this is the case, and to ensure the smooth running of the operation, all points including access and soil disposal should be looked at in very close detail.

Access in particular is very important, though there are now various sizes of mechanical digger to suit almost every need. The most common is a large digger, or JCB, and where this is the preferred option be sure to invite the JCB driver to visit the site, where a plan of action can be discussed and any likely problems can be solved.

Another popular method of excavation involves the use of smaller mechanical diggers. These can be hired on a daily basis without a driver and are very popular for small conversion and home extension works. Unlike home extension works, conversion work often requires working within very close proximity to the existing building. Where this is the case and where the use of this type of digger is the preferred option, make absolutely sure that there is enough room for the digger to carry out the job in hand successfully and without risk of harm to either the building or the digger operative.

Where there is a choice of excavation methods so there is also a choice with soil disposal. Every section of the building work should be planned carefully and the removal of any discharge from the site is no exception. The removal of any or all excavation materials should be planned meticulously. It is unlikely that the soil removed from underpinning or similar close proximity works will be suitable for the garden, so disposal will almost certainly be the best option.

BRICKS BELOW GROUND
Not all 'facing' bricks are suitable for use below ground level. Check with your supplier that the materials you plan to use are suitable for that purpose.

A garage floor base laid on hardcore with the foundation shown as a thickened base. Where this is the case, and depending upon the extent of the conversion work, a completely new foundation will almost certainly be required.

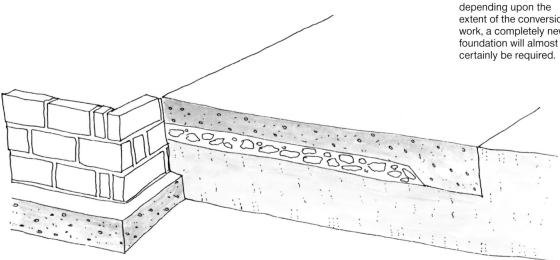

Groundworks

UNDERPINNING

Underpinning the existing foundations can be very tedious and also extremely strenuous. Only small sections of the existing foundations should be exposed at any one time, about a metre in length, and a trench should then be dug to the depth required by Building Control. This area beneath the existing foundations can then be filled with concrete as required before the next section is worked on in the same way.

It is unlikely that full details of the underpinning required will be shown on the building plans and these may only be determined during a site visit made by the local authority building inspector. During this pre-arranged visit the building inspector will inspect the exist-ing foundations (an area will have to be exposed prior to the visit for this purpose) and determine what action is required to bring the existing foundations up to scratch. For single-storey conversions the existing foundations may well be suitable. Where the conversion works include another storey to be built above the garage, then the ability of the existing foundations to carry this additional load will come into question.

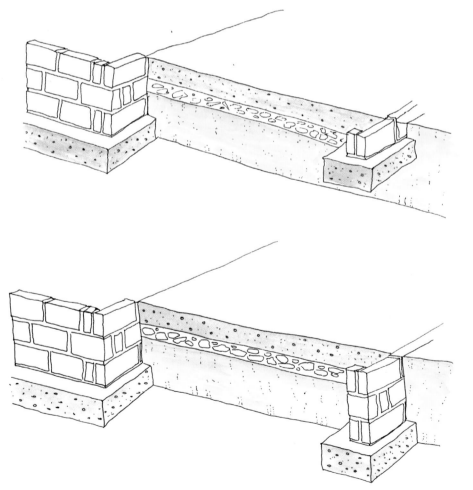

A garage floor laid on a hardcore base with a proper foundation, though not as deep as the house foundations. Depending upon the amount of conversion work this may be acceptable without further improvement.

A garage floor laid on a hardcore base where the foundations are a continuation of the existing house foundations. Where this is the case it is unlikely that additional foundation work will be required.

SETTING OUT

When the site is cleared of all obstructions and any vegetative materials the next thing to do is mark out the area for excavation. At this stage, accuracy is very important and an ability to follow the building plans will be essential. Where the excavations are under the existing walls, then setting out will only consist of datum levels. Where the excavations are for walls inside the existing building, then chalk lines will provide a very good guide.

For larger and more extensive conversion works involving a section of new-build where the excavations involve walls not yet built, even where they form an addition to the existing walls, then correct positioning and depth will be vital. It is only after the concrete foundations are laid that positional changes become both difficult and expensive and this may reflect on the overall success of the project as a whole. After setting out, check and double check the overall trench dimensions and then compare the positions against the approved plans.

At an early stage it is a good idea to mark out the excavation area with a line of sand showing the full extent of the excavation area, but before work starts in earnest a greater degree of accuracy will be required.

To set out the foundation trenches properly you will require a good spirit level, 1m or longer, a length of good building line and sufficient profile boards to the working details required. The profile boards will be used as guides to check levels such as the damp-proof course (DPC) level and finished floor level.

Before setting up the profile boards it is important to select a common level from which all measurements can be taken. As a general rule, in the building trade, the existing DPC will be the best guide and a datum peg should be set up at selected points away from the building to provide a permanent guide from which all levels can be taken.

A datum peg can be made easily from a length of wood, say 50mm × 50mm, and then hammered into the ground at a good enough depth to ensure stability. The top of the datum peg will be the reference point to be used for measurements and levels. Where the existing DPC is selected as the level, then the top of the datum peg will be levelled off with the DPC. Of course, you don't have to use the existing damp-proof level as a guide, you may prefer to use the existing floor level, and this is fine just as long as the guide you choose is on the existing building and the point remains constant.

Have you any previous experience of underpinning?

Groundworks

Position the datum peg at the furthest point from the existing building but close enough to the new excavation area to provide the necessary points of reference. Where the datum is placed too far from the excavation area it will prove difficult to work from and where it is positioned too close it may well get dislodged or moved and will need to be set up again. Even where the datum pegs are set in safe areas, free from disruption, they should be checked regularly to make sure the building level remains constant.

With the datum peg in position the newly made profile boards can be erected. The top of each profile board will be levelled up with the top of the datum peg as these boards will provide the guide to future wall positions. With the use of the builder's line the trenches to be excavated can be set out showing the finished wall positions.

The profile boards should be made from sturdy pieces of timber and, like the datum peg, must be set up close to, but not affecting, the excavation works. They should also be regularly checked to see that they are both level and square. The correct positioning of the datum peg will ensure the building is built level and the correct positioning of the profile boards will ensure that the building is built square, particularly its corners.

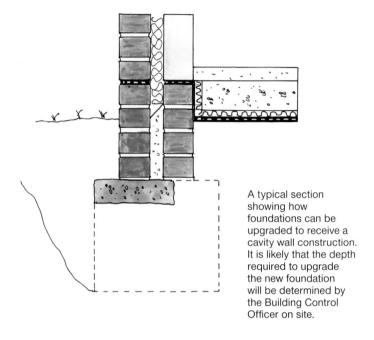

A typical section showing how foundations can be upgraded to receive a cavity wall construction. It is likely that the depth required to upgrade the new foundation will be determined by the Building Control Officer on site.

Allow adequate access on site for delivery lorries.

A good method for checking that the corners are square is with the use of a builder's square. Starting at the existing building, armed with the builder's square, a set of plans and working in conjunction with the newly set datum pegs, the profile boards can be set up. Attach the builder's line to the building at a point from which the levels have been taken and run the line to a point that is at least 1.5 m further than the proposed wall position. At this point the first profile board can be erected. Using the builder's square to ensure the new wall will run at right angles to the existing wall, a nail can be hammered into the top of the profile board showing the line of the new wall. It is from this nail that further measurements can be taken. Always double-check all lines and measurements before continuing. Measure twice and fix once. This process of setting up profile boards can be repeated where other new walls are proposed. When the builder's string lines are in position, the outline of the newbuild should be seen clearly. Where new corner walls are to be built and where the builder's lines cross, be sure to check these points are square before continuing.

From these outer string lines the internal walls can be measured and, adding nails to the top of the profile boards, lines can be set up showing the internal wall positions. The string lines should always run parallel and the gap between them should equal the wall thickness shown on the building plans. Now the outer lines showing the position of excavation must be added.

First check the required foundation width on the approved building plans, then deduct the wall thickness from that width. When divided by two this will give you the amount of overhang the foundations have when compared with walls. Using this measurement add further nails to the top of the profile boards. When string lines are attached the outline of the foundation trenches can be seen. Using these outer lines as a guide a trickle of sand can be poured on the ground along the line of the excavation works both internally and

externally. Then, leaving the profile in position for future reference, the string lines can be removed to allow clear, unobstructed access to the excavation area.

> **PLASTICIZER**
>
> A plasticizer can be used in mortar, it will add air and provide some protection from frost damage. It will, however, delay setting times.
>
> Do not use washing-up liquid. It does not have the qualities required for this process.

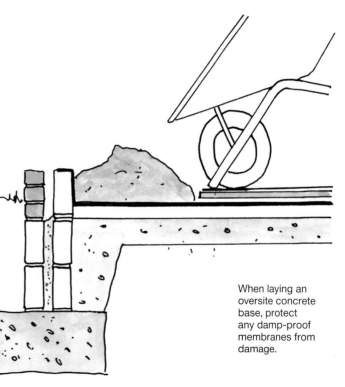

When laying an oversite concrete base, protect any damp-proof membranes from damage.

Groundworks

The builder's string line can be replaced at any time to check positions and then, after the concrete foundations are laid and the new walls built to DPC level the profile boards can be removed. Always leave the datum peg in position until the building work is complete.

FOUNDATIONS

As soon as the excavation works have been completed the work will need to be inspected by the local authority building inspector and you will be asked to give twenty-four hours' notice to Building Control for the inspection to be carried out before the foundation concrete can be laid. If, on inspection, the Building Inspector feels that the trench base is not secure or that the trench has not been excavated to a suitable standard to ensure the integrity and stability of the new foundation, then you may be required to make whatever improvements are necessary. This could include excavating to a more suitable depth where the foundations can be laid on a secure base.

When the trenches have been approved the arrangements for pouring the concrete can be put in place. The builder's lines will have been removed, though the profile boards should be left in place for the bricklayer to set up the wall positions.

The decision about the type of foundation suitable for this project will be shown on the building plans and the depth can be set out by driving stakes firmly and centrally into the base of the trenches with the top of the stake showing the top of the foundation concrete. Where the trenches are long these stakes should be set out at approximately 2m centres and then a short plank can be used to level off the concrete. To calculate accurately the finished level of the concrete foundation, measure down from the original point of reference, or the datum peg, using a gauge rod.

A JCB with or without driver can be hired for larger excavation works.

A gauge rod can be made from a length of timber with markings set on it showing brick levels. This method of measurement is widely used by bricklayers indicating the number of brick courses required and where the DPC is to be installed. For example, if the walls to be built in the footings (the walls below the DPC) are concrete blocks with a brick finish where the wall is visible, your gauge rod can be used for measurement. On the gauge rod the measurements will include the mortar bed used on each course. Thus the gauge rod will be set out as first a mortar bed, then a brick course, then another mortar bed, then another brick course, and so on. Working with a gauge rod will reduce the possibility of a split course of bricks or blocks.

You may find that by increasing the depth of foundations over and above that shown on the plans – never less than specified – you can lay the concrete foundation accurately to suit brick and block courses. A split course is where a brick or block is cut down in size and is permissible below ground level, and when built correctly should not affect the integrity of the wall. This can be avoided by setting the foundation depth according to the gauge rod so that bricks and blocks can be built in complete courses.

A typical concrete mix for foundations is 1:3:6 and consists of one part Portland cement (Portland cement is a complex, heat-treated mixture of lime, silicates and aluminium with iron oxides added) and nine parts ballast (already mixed at three parts sand and six parts gravel). When mixed with water the mixture undergoes a fairly rapid chemical reaction that transforms it into a hard, rock-like substance with great strength.

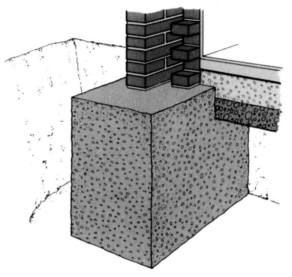

Trench fill foundation.

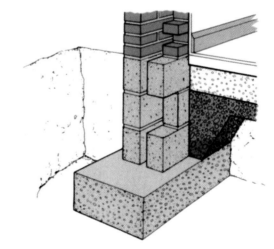

Strip foundations.

Groundworks

Small conversion and extension foundations can be mixed on site or delivered, ready mixed, to be poured into the foundation trenches to the depth required by the Building Inspector. A specified foundation depth may be shown on your building plans although this is flexible in that you can increase it (but it is unlikely you will be allowed to decrease it).

STRIP, TRENCH-FILL AND RAFT FOUNDATIONS

There are two common types of concrete foundation, each having benefits of their own. The first, and most popular, is a strip foundation. Set in the bottom of the trench at a minimum agreed depth, as specified on your building plans, the walls will be built centrally off the foundation to ensure stability. The second type, and also very popular, is a trench-fill foundation which is, as it sounds, a concrete foundation filling the trench to within a short distance of the top. Both foundation depths should be determined with the gauge rod in mind and must be approved by the Building Inspector.

One of the most important benefits to be gained from trench-filled foundations is that it is possible to build a new wall off the edge of the foundation and they are therefore ideal when building close to a boundary. Conversely, walls must be built centrally on strip foundations so that the building structure retains its integrity. One of the drawbacks with

trench-fill foundations is that where drainage pipes pass through the foundation, extra care must be taken to ensure that the pipes are not damaged. This will apply during the concrete pouring and is usually by way of padding around the pipe, giving it protection from the settling of the concrete.

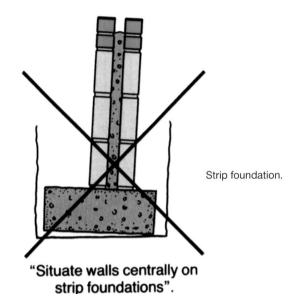

Strip foundation.

"Situate walls centrally on strip foundations".

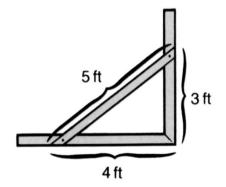

Builder's square.

5 ft

3 ft

4 ft

A third and much less common foundation is a raft foundation. Raft foundations are more likely to be used where the ground is unstable and where there is a risk of subsidence. Raft foundations will vary according to location and design but in general will consist of a layer of concrete, then before the concrete sets a reinforcing mesh will be added, then another layer of concrete is poured over. This method of layering can be repeated depending upon the design of the raft.

meet and this join would be a weak point in the foundation.

When you are mixing the concrete by hand at least one man should mix and pour while another levels off each load. For larger jobs pre-mixed concrete from a ready-mix supplier will save a lot of work and speed up the process. The concrete will be delivered to a mix you specify (1:3:6 is most common for foundations although ground conditions will

POURING CONCRETE FOUNDATIONS

Speed is the most important requirement when laying or pouring concrete. First mixing and then pouring the concrete should be a continuous process to ensure that each load bleeds in well with the previous load, maintaining the strength of the concrete. Do not pour in a load and then leave it for an hour or so before pouring in the next load. Concrete soon becomes dry and unworkable, and so a join could form where the two loads

dictate) and to a working consistency applicable to the circumstances. If the concrete can be poured directly into the footings all will be well but where the concrete has to be dumped onto a large plastic sheet and then wheel-barrowed to the trenches, ask the supplier about adding a retarder. This will give you a little 'working' time, usually a couple of hours, before the concrete starts to dry out.

Make sure all the tools to be used are suitable for the purpose. A good-quality spirit level such as the BMI Robust is essential.

Level off areas using a good 'straight edge'.

Groundworks

When you order concrete from a ready-mix supplier make sure you tell the supplier what the concrete is for, the area and depth you are filling and if the load is to be dumped on to a sheet or poured directly into the footings. Do not calculate how much concrete is required too exactly and always allow a little extra for error. If when the concrete is poured in you have some left over, the lorry driver will usually take it away for you. If you have some left over on the sheet and it cannot easily be used anywhere else on the site, spread it out as thinly as you can and leave it to dry. It can then be used as hardcore or ballast, on the oversite area, for example. Do not leave it in a huge lump to be broken up later.

BELOW-GROUND MASONRY

When you have finished the footings and the concrete has had at least a couple of days to set, or 'cure' to be precise, the bricklayer can come in and build the walls up to damp-proof level. These walls will generally be built in blockwork and brickwork, or just brickwork, but make sure that the materials you use (blocks, bricks and cement) are suitable for walls below ground level. Not all materials are suitable for this purpose and will degenerate very quickly due to the extra moisture associated with being below ground.

After the foundations are laid you can use the gauge rod to calculate the number of blocks and bricks required for building these walls up to DPC level.

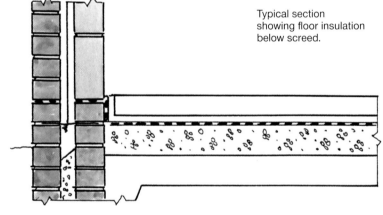

Typical section showing floor insulation below screed.

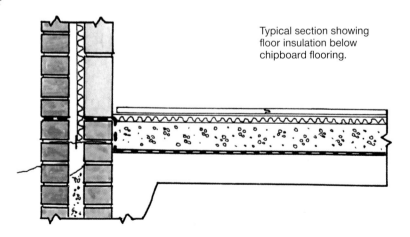

Typical section showing floor insulation below chipboard flooring.

DAMP-PROOF COURSE

To prevent dampness rising from the ground upwards and causing damage to both the internal and external walls of the new building work a damp-proof course, or DPC, must be installed. The DPC will be built into both walls and bedded on with mortar. Where the new DPC abuts any existing walls it will be dressed into the existing DPC to provide a continuous and preventative barrier. The DPC should be at least 150 mm above ground level and where this is not possible, when you are building into a bank or similar higher ground, all precautions must be taken to ensure that water penetration to the internal walls is prevented.

Groundworks

STEP-BY-STEP SUMMARY

1. Check the location of incoming services such as gas and electricity.
2. Dig trial holes alongside existing foundations to determine their depth and suitability.
3. Set up your 'levels' using the existing DPC as a guide.
4. Cover up open excavations overnight or when they are unattended.
5. Using datum pegs as a guide lay the foundation concrete to the depth required.
6. Build below-ground walls up to DPC level and backfill to ground level.

POINT OF GOOD BUILDING PRACTICE 5
Always protect cavity insulation and the open cavity from wayward mortar. Keeping the cavity clean will prevent it from being bridged, which would increase the possibility of dampness inside the building.

WALLS AND LINTELS

Converting a garage into living accommodation will, almost inevitably, involve the existing garage walls remaining *in situ* while being upgraded to meet building regulations approval. To achieve this there are several sections of the existing construction that must be looked at closely. These will include the structural capability of the walls, as well as the foundations, the thermal capabilities of the walls and, where any part of the structure needs upgrading, will include windows, doors and internal walls.

Where the existing wall forms part of the house structure and the garage is an integral part of the building. it is likely that the walls and foundations will be suitable for conversion. Where the garage is an addition to the existing house. then the walls, and possibly the foundations, may not be suitable for domestic purposes without upgrading. The building plans will show the existing structure and what methods of construction are required to bring the new work up to scratch. This may include the forming of a completely new cavity wall structure using any of the wide variety of available construction methods to meet the building regulations requirements, or it may involve minimal work – this will all depend upon the existing structure.

A cavity wall construction can be formed as a blockwork structure built off the foundations or it can be formed as a abuts another building and the wall forms part of the boundary, must be looked at in a different light. There are specific requirements and guidelines for the developer to follow ensuring their works do not impinge on a neighbouring property or put its structure at risk.

Wall construction must be carried out in a professional manner with good clean cavities, suitable and well-spaced wall ties and sufficient bearings for lintels over openings.

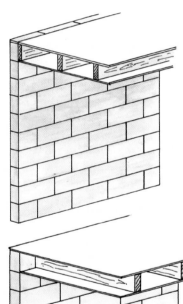

Non-load-bearing wall.

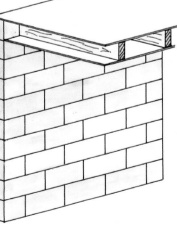

Load-bearing wall.

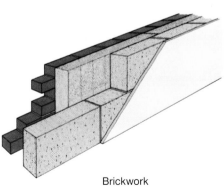

Brickwork
50mm 'Rockwool'
cavity insulation
100mm insulation blocks.

73

Walls and Lintels

Where openings are formed in the cavity wall for windows and doors, adequate damp-proof protection will be needed as well as thermal protection to retain heat in the building and therefore reduce the risk of damp.

Lintels and RSJs may be required where the existing structure is limited and these will need to be installed correctly with the correct bearing for support, the correct damp-proofing above and to either side of the opening and, where it is not included, insulation. RSJs are more commonly used internally as load-bearing supports and these must be fire-proofed.

Every aspect of the wall construction will be covered by building regulations and it is essential that the work is carried out properly, however small the project is.

STARTING WORK

A garage conversion can be spotted quite easily, on occasion, but the very best conversions blend in well with the existing property. The new walls should have been designed and built to blend in well with the existing walls and the roof structure should also blend in. As far as wall construction is concerned it is unlikely that you will have had a choice of materials from which to build your new walls, because the planning officer is likely to stipulate that the materials you use match the existing building as closely as possible. Even where planning permission is not required, finding a suitable match to the existing wall construction will inevitably produce the best results. Bricks, and old bricks in particular, seldom match exactly and where the original brick makers no longer produce the same bricks, or are no longer in business, trying to copy the exact bricks may be difficult. When you have to choose a substitute brick it is important to consider what effect weathering will have on it and what the brick will look like in a few years' time. If a near match cannot be found and you decide to use a brick that you believe is complementary to the existing bricks, take a sample to your planning department for their approval (if planning permission forms part of the approval) before you make a purchase or start any building work.

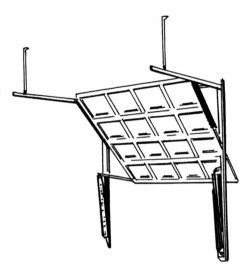

Up-and-over garage door with side springs.

Support the garage door at all corners before releasing the spring mechanism.

Bricks are the most popular material used in house building today and date back at least 5,000 years, to the ancient Egyptians, but they are not the only material in use. Natural stonework, for example, dates back to long before the invention of the brick but this extremely attractive and desirable product has become expensive to use in modern construction and is not easy to build with. To satisfy demand and to retain appearances where existing stone buildings are common, a preformed, manmade block with a stone appearance is used. These blocks are less expensive to build with, are readily available and provide a suitable alternative to natural stone. Another popular wall construction in use today includes concrete blocks with a concrete render finish. These, and many others, all add to the diversity of choice available to designers. In fact, construction technology of the modern home has changed such a great deal during the last fifty years, with damp-proofing, cavity wall insulation and other energy-saving innovations playing a major role in wall design, that only minor improvements can be expected in the immediate future.

Where a garage door is to be removed and a window of the same width is fitted, leaving a panel below the window to be constructed, this can be used as a high-light section differing from the existing structure. For example, where the existing structure is brickwork, perhaps a stonework section may be suitable and vice versa. The range of possibilities is great and the end result of making a feature of this section of wall can be quite outstanding.

Cavity insulation with wall ties in place.

REMOVING THE GARAGE DOOR

Up-and-Over Door

An up-and-over door works on a pivotal basis where the door is opened from the lower half to swing up through its own axis, to rest horizontally inside the garage. There are a huge number of both types and designs, from steel to wood to fibreglass. Some have springs on either side of the door and some have a central overhead spring designed to carry the weight of the door through its movement.

To remove an up-and-over door the tension of these springs must be released and the springs removed. In the majority of cases the spring pressure is loaded when the door is in a closed position and it is at its minimum pressure when the door is fully open. It seems sensible, therefore, to remove the springs and cables when the door is in an open position but the very nature of the door may well make this almost impossible due to lack of room in which to work.

Where possible the door should be opened and, because the door is supported by the spring mechanism, cradled so that it is fixed *in situ*. Perhaps the best way to do this is to fix timber struts under the open door at either corner, to bear the weight when the springs are removed.

When the struts are in place loosen off the springs using a spanner. When the tension is off the door the supports can be removed and the door lowered through its channels into the closed position. The spring mechanism and associate wiring can now be removed and the tracks loosened to free the door.

This is a very tricky exercise that can be fraught with problems and must never be undertaken by the unprepared. Garage doors are heavy and bulky items, and springs and tension can be dangerous when handled without the utmost respect. Help will be required for both manhandling and securing the area.

When the garage door and the fittings are removed, then the framework can also be removed to leave the door opening ready for the next stage of work.

Up-and-over door with overhead spring loading.

Roller Door

A roller door, whether electric or manual, operates on the same principle as an up-and-over door in that it operates by tension, but it differs in the fact that it rolls up as opposed to swinging into the garage. To remove a roller door the best way will probably be when it is open. This is because the door is already rolled up and it will be easier to remove and relocate in this mode. The tension for a roller door is also spring-operated, but, unlike up-and-over doors, the spring is above the door and is concealed when it is in a rolled-up position. The tension must be released before the door can be removed. I believe the best method to release the tension is to loosen the bolts holding the central rod. Before doing this put a tie or belt or something similar around the door, because it will loosen when the tension is off.

When the tie is in place, gently loosen the securing bolts either side until you hear the spring unwind. The noise will be distinctive. Do not unscrew the bolts completely. They will almost certainly be holding the door onto its brackets.

Finally, unscrew the end bolts and slide the door up on its brackets and then lower it to the floor. Roller doors are very heavy and help will be needed at both ends. Where an electrical door opener is installed, be sure to disconnect the electrical works before attempting to remove the door.

CAVITY WALL CONSTRUCTION

All the external walls of new buildings, and this includes windows and doors, must meet with stringent building regulation requirements before approval will be given. Cavity wall construction, which has been designed to provide protection from damp penetration and reduce heat loss from the building, consists of a decorative outer wall, a cavity (filled or partially filled with an insulator) and an internal wall.

First remove the garage door.

Walls and Lintels

Damp penetration is one of the most serious of building defects and can cause extensive damage to the structure, both inside and out. When a cavity wall is built properly it should not permit damp penetration, even in exposed areas, and when it does it is usually owing to the cavity being bridged. The commonest form of cavity bridging allowing damp to penetrate the building is as a result of mortar droppings left on wall ties, or where mortar has dropped down the cavity during construction work.

Another major factor requiring consideration is where the external walls must comply with current building regulations concerning heat loss. Every external wall structure, and this will include windows and doors, must meet accepted thermal requirements or 'U' values, from which the building's energy use can be calculated. To assist the retention of heat within the building a variety of wall structures can be considered. The internal wall can be built using insulation blocks with solid or fibre insulation added to the cavity. Similarly, the wall can be of timber construction. There are, suitably, numerous variations on this theme with the one single aim of keeping energy loss to a minimum and producing a cavity wall that meets all the statutory requirements.

MORTAR

In the dictionary 'mortar' is defined as a mixture of sand and cement used to join stones and bricks together. In fact it is far more important than that. A good cement mortar is essential to achieve the right finish and give lasting strength to your walls. Portland cement and soft sand at a ratio of about one part cement to four parts sand is a widely used recipe for walls both above and below ground. Non-hydraulic and semi-hydraulic lime can be added for workability, strength and to lighten the mortar, with other additives including a plasticizer for workability and a colourant to add colour.

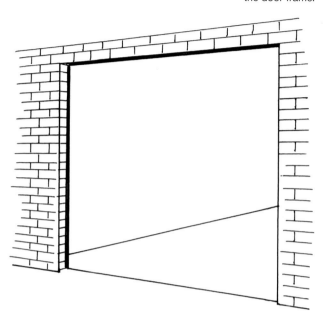

Second step: remove the door frame.

Where a template is required position it accurately before building around it.

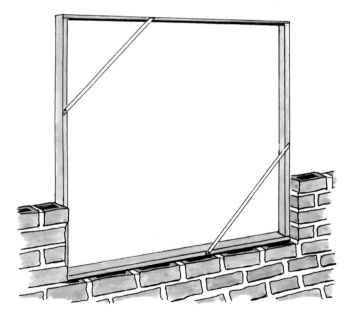

The mixture should not be too wet, or the bricklayer will struggle to lay it as a bed for the bricks. If it is too weak (too much sand) the joints may crumble away and if it is too strong (too much cement) the joints may crack. Enough water should be added to produce a good dropping consistency off the trowel, allowing it to spread easily and providing enough time for the brick to be laid to a line and level. Where the bricks, the sand or the weather increase the drying out time, making life difficult for the bricklayer, a plasticizer can be added. A good local brickie will know local sand grades, when best to lay the bricks in terms of the weather, and the strength of mixture most suitable for the bricks you use. Where it is necessary to build external walls during inclement weather, then adequate protection, sacking sheets or similar, must be provided to prevent the water in the mortar from freezing.

Where mortar is concerned there are three simple points to be given close consideration for producing the very best brickwork:

- use an experienced local bricklayer;
- keep the sand covered when not in use;
- store the cement in a dry area, off the ground, and use within a short time. Cement does not generally store well, even in dry areas.

Finally, mortar can be deceptive as it dries out and getting the right mix to match the existing building may be tricky and may not always be achievable.

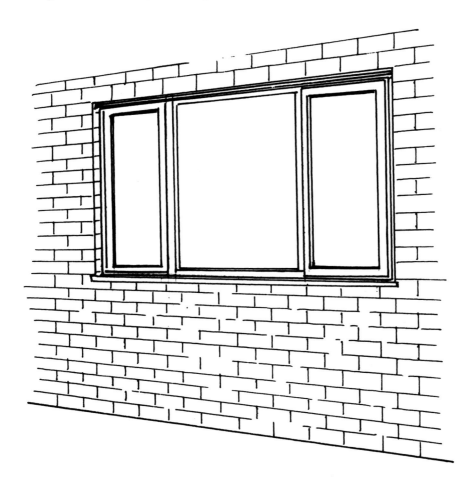

Fit window in place to complete the front elevation.

CAVITY WALL INSULATION

With fuel costs steadily, even rapidly, rising annually, energy-saving is money-saving. In England and Wales there are clear guidelines where walls and windows must achieve a minimum in energy saving, and these are calculated in 'U' values. The 'U' value of a wall shows the thermal transmittance (heat transfer) through a wall when outside temperatures differ from inside temperatures. To limit the heat loss through the fabric of the building, cavity wall insulation can be built into it in various forms.

Standard forms of insulation include using insulation batts 50 mm thick for filling the cavity and expanded polystyrene sheets 25 mm thick attached to the inner wall using special clips. Good site care is necessary to ensure that the installation process is carried out successfully. Where the cavity insulation fills the cavity all mortar droppings should be prevented from falling down the cavity and the insulation batts must be protected against wet weather. Where the expanded polystyrene sheets are used, they must be attached firmly to the internal wall and not left flapping about freely. Installation problems may arise where the wall ties are fitted badly or irregularly, causing the slabs to be chopped about unnecessarily.

The installation of cavity insulation will be carried out by the bricklayer as he builds the walls and it must be kept clean and dry at all times. Store the insulation in a dry place until it is used and always cover an unfinished wall overnight as a protection against dampness.

WALL TIES

To build a strong, stable cavity wall, wall ties must be fitted at regular intervals. There are several types on the market all designed to add strength to cavity walls in particular, and to restrict water penetration where the wall tie forms a bridge connecting the outer wall to the inner wall. Poor installation, however, where a wall tie is not level and slopes toward the inner wall, can provide the bridge necessary for rainwater, after it has soaked the outer wall, to transfer the

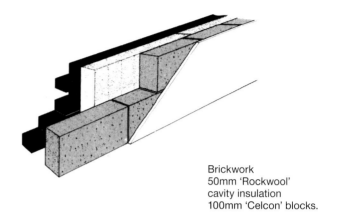

Brickwork
50mm 'Rockwool'
cavity insulation
100mm 'Celcon' blocks.

dampness to the inner wall. Your choice of wall tie may well be dictated by the type of cavity insulation you use but with all of them the wall ties must be kept clean and free of mortar droppings during construction.

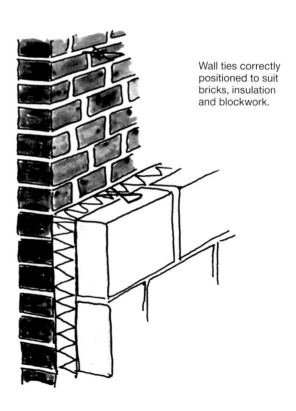

Wall ties correctly positioned to suit bricks, insulation and blockwork.

Where an existing single-skin wall is being upgraded to a double-skin wall, ties will almost certainly be required to strengthen the structure. This may include drilling and screwing wall ties at required intervals.

WEEP VENTS

Where water penetration occurs through the outer wall and into the cavity area, it must be diverted to areas where it can exit through weep vents. When water does enter the cavity, often as a result of heavy or driving rain, it will inevitably travel downwards. Where the wall has openings for windows and doors, this water will meet a barrier formed by the lintel. In the past this water has been known to cause damp problems around these openings. To rectify this, weep vents should be installed at regular intervals through which this water can be dispersed. Similarly, where cavity trays are installed to divert water within the cavity, an exit strategy must be built in using weep vents.

INDENTS AND PROFILES

Where a new wall abuts the existing wall, a proper join must be made to ensure stability. There are two principal ways of carrying out this process. The first is by cutting indents into the existing wall, forming a mortice-and-tenon-style joint, and then building the new wall into the indents. The second is by fixing profiles against the existing wall and building the attachments in as the new wall is built. This connection will also provide a 'bridge' where dampness can penetrate through to the inside walls, so a vertical DPC must be fitted. Using a disc cutter or angle grinder hired from your local hire shop, you can cut a line through the wall you are building into, approximately central to the cavity of the new adjoining wall, for the full height of the building. A DPC can then be inserted, thus providing a continuous barrier against damp.

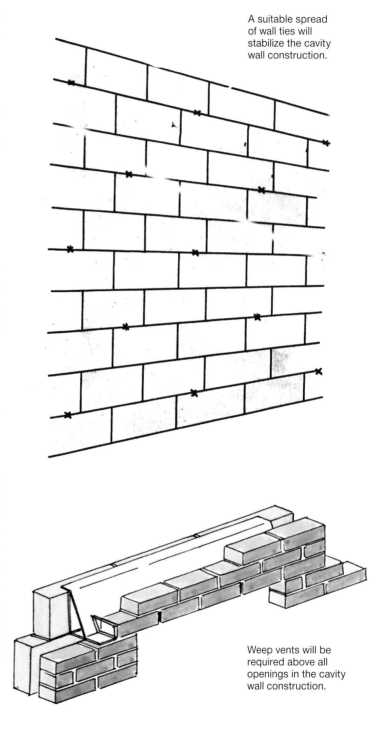

A suitable spread of wall ties will stabilize the cavity wall construction.

Weep vents will be required above all openings in the cavity wall construction.

WALL PLATE

When a new wall reaches roof level, be it a single-storey building or two-storey building, a softwood wall plate will be fitted, for both resting the roof timbers on it and securing the roof to it. In the majority of cases the wall plate will be bedded onto the inner wall and then secured with mild steel galvanized restraint straps, set at a maximum of 2 m centres and starting no more than 450 mm from corners. To ensure that the roof can be built geometrically, the wall plates, bedded onto opposite walls, must be level and square with each other.

PARTY WALLS

Where the garage to be converted adjoins another garage or building and the garage wall forms part of the boundary to a neighbouring property, then extra care must be taken to follow the strict guidelines in place (see Party Wall Act 1996). Use of this wall as a load-bearing wall for either additional walling or simply as a lintel support must meet fully with building regulation requirements and any invasive work will almost certainly have to include written permission from your neighbour. Verbal permission will not be acceptable and may invoke problems should the properties be sold at a later date.

Apart from the structural risk element of work involving neighbouring properties and party walls, the risk of fire should be a particular consideration. Of course, these precautions should be shown clearly in the approved building plans but it is essential in these circumstances that work does not commence until all the approvals are obtained and permission is granted.

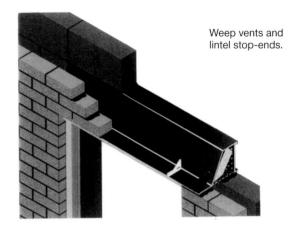

Weep vents and lintel stop-ends.

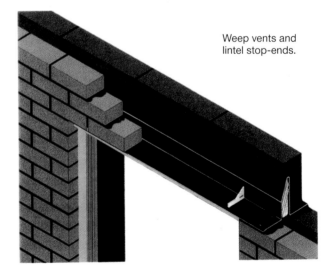

Weep vents and lintel stop-ends.

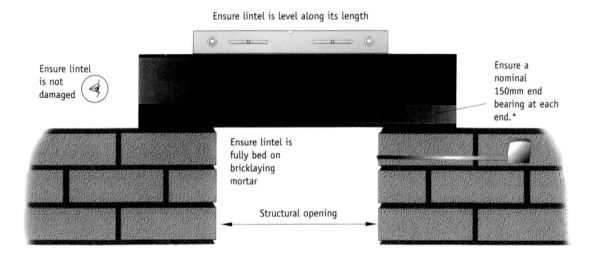

Ensure lintel is level along its length

Ensure lintel is not damaged

Ensure a nominal 150mm end bearing at each end.*

Ensure lintel is fully bed on bricklaying mortar

Structural opening

In cavity walls, raise inner and outer leaves supported by lintel together.†

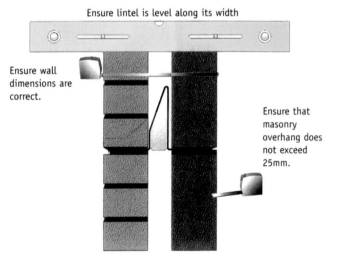

Ensure lintel is level along its width

Ensure wall dimensions are correct.

Ensure that masonry overhang does not exceed 25mm.

Masonry above lintels should be allowed to cure before applying floor or roof loads.

Installing a Catnic lintel.

LINTELS AND ROLLED STEEL JOISTS (RSJs)

A lintel is a horizontal beam, historically made from stone and later forming the shape of a brick arch, but now more commonly seen as galvanized steel or precast concrete. The lintel is built into a wall as the building progresses and provides a support for masonry above an opening such as a window or door. To function properly the lintel must be installed correctly and should not be damaged in any way prior to the installation, as this damage may result in the lintel failing in its task. It will be bedded on mortar, onto both the inner and outer walls as they have been built up together. For lintels, building regulations are particularly clear about *three* specific points:

• The lintel must have an end bearing, resting on each supporting wall, of at least 150 mm each end.
• The thermal bridging requirements (R-values) must be achieved.
• The water penetration, a result of water travelling down the cavity, must be directed to the external wall and the weep vents.

To satisfy the second and third points lintel manufacturers have amended the design of their product so that the lintels are both insulated to meet the requirements but also designed, like a cavity tray, to direct downward water to the outside wall. To assist this final point additional precautions must be taken to allow this water to exit through weep holes built into the external wall at either end of the lintel, to include the proper installation of stop ends to direct moisture toward the weep holes.

An RSJ or a Universal Beam may be specified where extra-large openings in walls occur that are considered outside the scope of standard lintels. These strong beams can be purchased in a variety of lengths and cross-sections appropriate for almost any circumstance. Where a beam is required it is likely that Building Control will request structural calculations to prove the ability of the beam to carry the load to be imposed upon it. Unlike standard steel lintels these beams can be extremely heavy, putting an extra emphasis on installation.

The beam must be bedded onto special load-bearing padstones or engineering bricks, and in some cases steel plates, in order to spread an imposed load with the potential to crush standard bricks and blocks over a wider area.

Where an RSJ is installed there will be specific fire protection precautions that must be followed. However strong these joists are, and their inclusion is only required as a major structural element to the building, they are susceptible to fire damage.

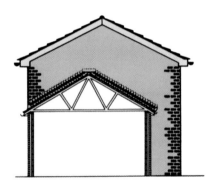

Type 'X' cavity tray.

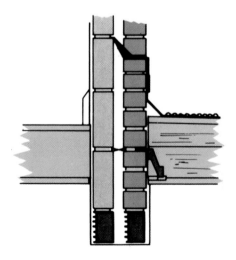

Type 'E' cavity tray.

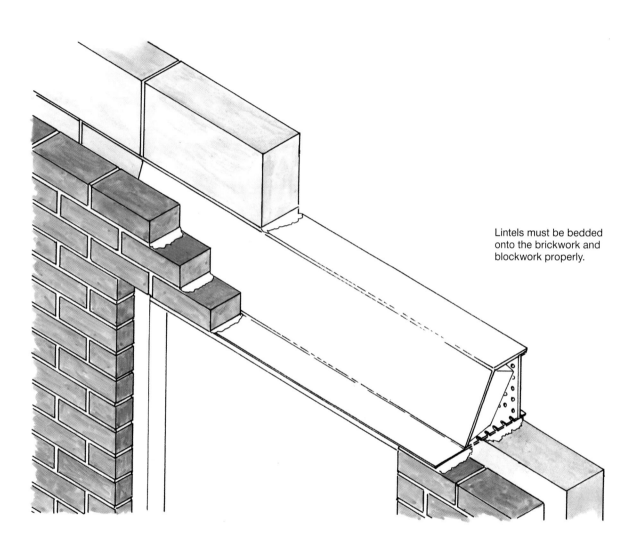

Lintels must be bedded
onto the brickwork and
blockwork properly.

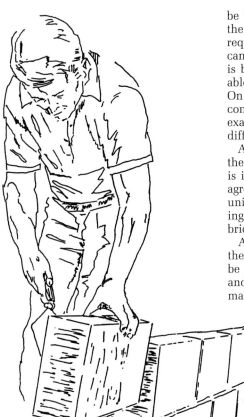

be 'day rate' and, as the term denotes, the bricklayer will carry out the work required and will be paid by the day. This can be a risky method of payment and is best used when supervision is available, reducing the risk of time-wasting. On the other hand when a garage or any conversion work is complex, putting an exact price on the work involved may be difficult.

Any quotes received will not include the supply of materials or plant hire. Nor is it likely to include (unless otherwise agreed) making templates for window units, erecting pole scaffolding or erecting gable end rafters where gable end brickwork is involved.

A good working relationship with all the tradesmen is required and there must be a clear understanding about what is and is not included in the price. All the materials must be discussed and they must be available on site when the bricklayer arrives to start.

BRICKLAYING

One of the oldest types of tradesman in the business, the bricklayer is responsible for the most visible part of your new building work. For this reason alone hiring an experienced, local bricklayer is essential. The 'brickie' will quote you for the job as a whole, or to carry out the work on a day rate basis, according to the degree of difficulty involved. A garage conversion may require only a small amount of bricklaying, or it may be a major project. Whichever is the case the bricklayer will generally quote using one of two methods. The first will be on a fixed price and will include all of the setting work, the installation of cavity insulation, setting up and building in door and window frames where required and, where necessary, the bedding on of the wall plate. The second method will

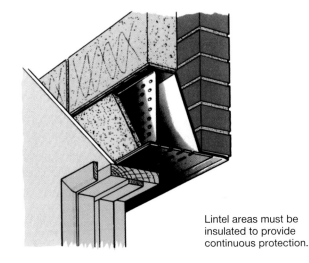

Lintel areas must be insulated to provide continuous protection.

SCAFFOLDING

The technical term used in the trade when referring to the height of walls during construction is the 'lift'. The 'lift' is the height at which scaffolding is required for tradesmen such as bricklayers and roofers to work from. For example, when a wall reaches the first lift height the bricklayer will require scaffolding to stand on so that the building can be built up to the next lift. Similarly, when the walls are built up to the second lift then a further level is required to put the roof on.

The scaffolding referred to in this example is called pole scaffolding where poles, or 'standards', are raised vertically and lateral poles, called ledgers, are bolted on horizontally. There are two types of pole scaffolding commonly in use. The first is a 'putlog' scaffold where special short poles with one end flattened off, called putlogs, are built into the walls as a support for the planks off which the builders will work. The whole scaffold is then braced at regular intervals through openings in the wall (windows, for example) for stability. The second type of pole scaffold is an 'independent' scaffold, almost free-standing, where two rows of standards are raised vertically and then bolted together with ledgers. This second type may appear to be free-standing but all scaffold must be tied into the building at regular intervals. Pole scaffolding of this type must be erected by highly skilled professionals as there are very stringent safety measures by which to abide.

Catnic CN lintels, suitable for internal partitions and load-bearing walls.

Pre-stressed concrete lintels must be built in correctly. Many will display markings showing which way up to install the lintel.

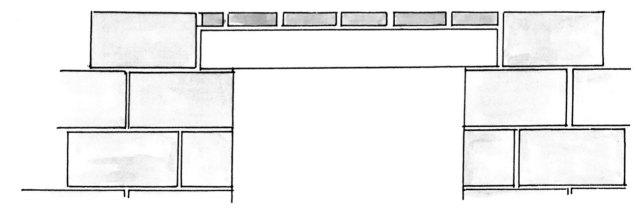

Walls and Lintels

SCAFFOLD HIRE

The height of your finished conversion will determine the type of scaffold you will require for the work to be carried out safely and successfully. Where the height is less than 8 ft, then trestles and planks are an option. These can be hired from your local hire shop and erected by the bricklayer during construction.

If the extension height exceeds 8 ft, or if the tradesmen request it, then pole scaffolding is likely to be the safest option. Professional supply-and-fit scaffolders are a must and they can be found in your local *Yellow Pages*. They will quote you for scaffolding the whole project, including additional lifts, and will then deliver and erect the lifts as required. Needless to say, close organizing with the scaffolders and the tradesmen will go a long way to ensuring that the project can continue without delays.

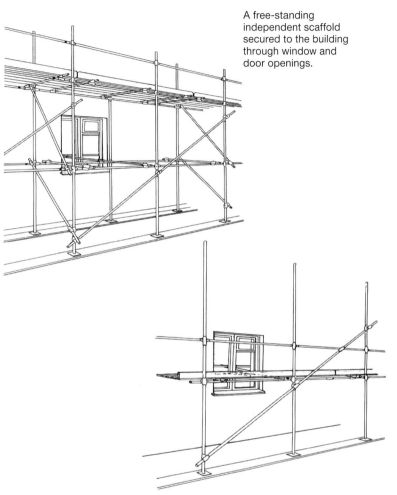

A free-standing independent scaffold secured to the building through window and door openings.

A putlog-style scaffold secured to the building through window and door openings.

STEP-BY-STEP SUMMARY

1. Check the existing garage wall construction to see how it can be best upgraded to meet your requirements.
2. Lintels installed in new walling may require weep vents to disperse dampness that falls down the cavity.
3. Removing the garage door could be a very tricky operation. Make sure you are fully aware of the operating mechanism whilst it is being removed and that there is sufficient assistance to carry out the work safely.
4. Where the garage is built along a boundary the wall may be shared with a neighbour – a party wall. Special care must be taken, and permission sought, when considering building on or against a party wall.
5. Where external walls are built during inclement weather, protection must be provided to prevent the water in the mortar from freezing.
6. Up-and-over garage doors may best be removed when they are fixed in a closed position.
7. Roller doors may best be removed when in a rolled-up or open position.
8. Scaffolding or trestles will be required for building the new walls.

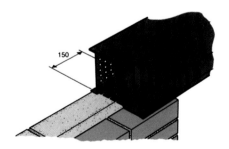

Minimum 150mm end bearings for all lintels.

> **POINT OF GOOD BUILDING PRACTICE 6**
> All lintels must have a minimum bearing of 150 mm. Where possible the lintel should be bedded on a full block and full brick.

DOOR AND WINDOW FRAMES

One of the more important decisions to be made during the planning process is the selection of door and window frames. The range of windows currently available from suppliers is vast, with a multitude of styles from which to choose including top-hung, side-hung, sash and tilt windows. The success of the project will depend largely upon their correct style, size and positioning. Initially, the Planning Department will take particular interest in whether any windows and doors meet with their rules. These rules will include privacy for neighbouring properties and proximity to existing boundaries. Building Control, on the other hand, will look at the window and door frames from a completely different perspective. Their brief will involve fire safety, the loss of energy or heat, ventilation and adequate light for habitable rooms. These are all areas for potential problems and must be addressed before approval is given.

The glazed area of each window is important because it will let in the sunlight we require but it will also let out heat. Double and triple glazing are available as energy-saving options if required. New bathrooms and toilets attract the closest inspection, where you will find

that ventilation is high on the list of priorities. Building regulations stipulate a minimum area of window opening for any habitable room to be at least one-twentieth of that room's floor area plus background ventilation, with a proportion of the primary ventilation at least 1.75 m above floor level. Background ventilation, generally fitted into the window frame in the shape of a trickle vent, will provide a source of constant and additional ventilation as an aid to reducing the risk of condensation.

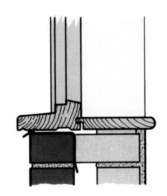

Vertical DPC to all reveals.

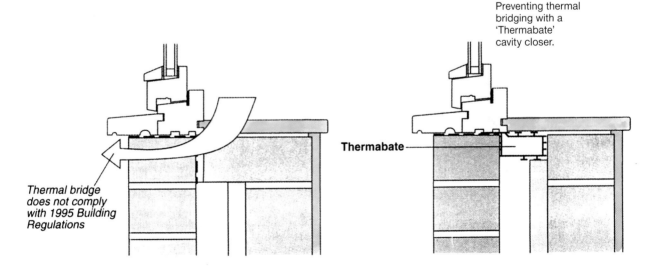

Thermal bridge does not comply with 1995 Building Regulations

Preventing thermal bridging with a 'Thermabate' cavity closer.

Thermabate

Door and Window Frames

UNGLAZED WINDOW FRAMES

It is standard building practice for the bricklayer to build unglazed window frames into walls as they progress. Before installation, wooden frames, including freshly sawn areas, should be stained or painted with primer and undercoated, then covered with sheeting as a protection against mortar damage. Frame ties (galvanized or stainless steel are the most common) will be screwed into the frames at regular intervals and then bedded into the mortar joints as the walls are built up.

WINDOW TEMPLATES

Unlike unglazed window frames, new made-to-measure windows are best installed after the walls are built. Building expensive hardwood or double-glazed units into new walls can be a very risky practice indeed, with a serious possibility of damage. If this is likely, then the best and most popular solution to this problem is to make, or get your carpenter to make, templates for the bricklayer to build the new walls around. The templates can then be removed and discarded and the new windows installed when all the construction work is completed. Each template will be made according to the size of the window as specified by your window manufac-

Vertical DPC with energy-saving cavity closer included

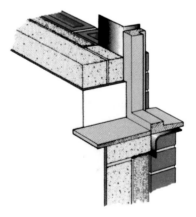

Vertical damp course.

turer. Here I must add a strong word of caution: the templates used by the bricklayer must be accurate. When the wall is built and the time has come to fit the new windows, if the opening is too small or excessively large, then this can cause major constructional problems, holding up the project for some time until it is sorted out.

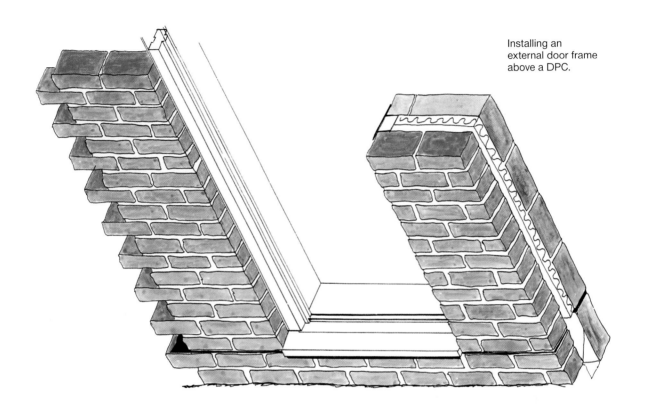

Installing an
external door frame
above a DPC.

Door and Window Frames

THERMAL BRIDGING

In recent years, the insulation of domestic buildings has come a long way but it has come to light that there is a possible weak area, around the windows and the doors. Here a 'bridge' connection where the cold outer wall adjoins the warm inner wall can be formed. On a cold day, for instance, the warm air inside the house will always travel to the colder outside air. This is called thermal conductivity and the risk of condensation is increased greatly when there is a significant difference between the colder external air and warmer internal air and, if left unchecked, it could lead to mould growth internally.

To help solve this problem, and as a guide for both manufacturers and their customers, a chart has been produced for the purpose of calculating the insulation potential or resistance of fittings in close proximity to a bridge. This chart shows the R-values, or resistance values, to be achieved. In an attempt to achieve the required R-values and therefore meet building regulation requirements in one area, above the openings, the hollow part of lintels (because they are often situated in the direct vicinity of a bridge) have been filled with insulation. This insulation has been found to improve the respective R-values of lintels and, by using this as a guide, can be of great help when purchasing lintels in the open market. The R-values are clearly shown in the manufacturer's literature so this can easily and accurately be compared against the R-values of competitors' lintels, thus allowing the purchaser more choice. Inevitably, the architect will specify certain lintels on the approved building plans and will have taken the lintels' suitability into consideration.

Another area of concern for thermal bridging and another area where the cavity is closed are the reveals around windows and doors, for example. To counter this thermal bridging products incorporating a DPC and appropriate insulation can be installed to reduce the risk of condensation and mould.

'Catnic' wall plate straps.

Ensure window and door frames are installed correctly.

VERTICAL DPC

As previously discussed, to prevent dampness rising from the ground a suitable DPC can be installed. This same method of protection against damp penetration can be applied to window and door openings in walls. Where the external and internal walls are joined together, at the 'reveals' around windows and doors, water penetration is possible and indeed likely, so a vertical damp-proof barrier must be installed during construction as a preventative measure. An insulated cavity closer can be used, tackling both the problems of damp penetration and heat loss through thermal bridging at the same time.

DOOR FRAMES

Access to the new garage conversion from the existing building may be formed internally, so there may be no need for an external door. Where an external door is to be fitted with or without a door cill, the choices will include softwood, hardwood and uPVC. The decision may well be determined by the existing window and door frames. Softwood frames can be built directly into the wall as it progresses, whereas hardwood frames and uPVC frames may be best installed after the building work is finished, to reduce the risk of damage. Where this is the case, as with the window frames, a template can be built to ensure the opening left in the wall is suitable to receive the door frame when the time comes.

Typical window section without suitable cavity closers in place.

Window and door templates can be built in during construction, then replaced when the building work is complete.

Door and Window Frames

Softwood door frames are commonly made from 100 mm [x] 75 mm softwood with a rebate for the door. When the frame is built into the new wall frame, ties will be secured to the frame at regular intervals, at least three each side; these will then be built into the wall as it progresses, bedded securely into the mortar joints.

Entrance doors, front and rear, will invariably open into the building whereas doors opening onto a balcony or to a garden area may well open outwards. To prevent rainwater penetration, a galvanized water bar will be fitted into the hardwood cill, set at a point approximately central to the bottom of the door. When the door is fitted, the bottom can be rebated over the water bar as required. All timber frames should be treated or primed and undercoated before installation, with the hardwood cill doubly protected and covered against mortar or traffic damage.

STEP-BY-STEP SUMMARY

1. When softwood windows are installed by the bricklayer, appropriate fixings must be provided.
2. Window templates should be made following accurate dimensions supplied by the window manufacturer.
3. To reduce the risk of thermal bridging around window and door openings ,lintels and vertical DPCs must be suitable for this purpose.
4. Only fit new doors into new frames. Do not try to reuse old frames.

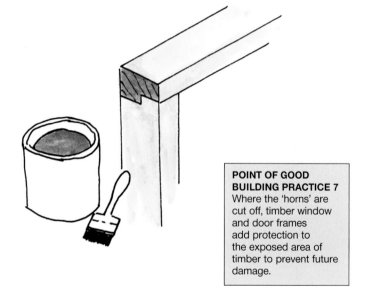

POINT OF GOOD BUILDING PRACTICE 7
Where the 'horns' are cut off, timber window and door frames add protection to the exposed area of timber to prevent future damage.

FLOORING

Floor construction for domestic building and conversion works will almost certainly fall into three distinct categories and the finished floor of the converted garage will inevitably replicate this, unless site circumstances demand otherwise. The first and most popular option is the ground-supported concrete floor. This is simply a concrete slab laid on the cleared oversite area, insulated to reduce heat loss and finished with a concrete screed. The second, not so common in modern homes, is the suspended wooden floor. This was very popular in post- and pre-war houses and consists of a concrete slab laid on the cleared oversite at a low level, where timber joists are inserted and a wooden floor is then secured to the timber joists. The third newer option, growing in popularity as a direct result of its easy installation, is the suspended beam and block floor. This is a duplicate of the suspended wooden floor construction where precast concrete beams are used instead of timber joists, with concrete blocks laid between the beams and a screed floor to finish off. The floor you install will be shown on the building plans but it is important that you look at all the possibilities before making a choice.

Where (and in many cases this is the rule and not the exception) the garage floor is stable, secure and will provide a

'Synthaprufe' damp proof membrane.

solid base to build off, then the differences between the existing floor level and the proposed floor level will be an important factor. As a result of modern construction where the domestic floor levels are expected to be higher than the ground level to reduce damp and the existing garage floor level is at ground level, a differential often arises. The size of this differential will dictate what flooring decisions are made. Where the difference between the existing floor level and the garage floor level is large, then the list of alternatives increases; when the difference is only slight, then the list of alternatives decreases.

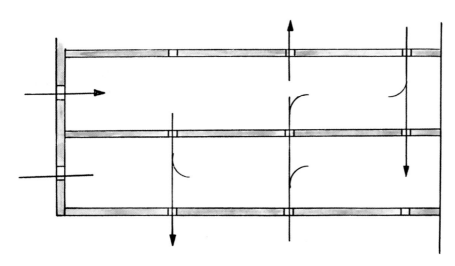

To prevent damage from moisture and fungi, adequate movement of 'free' air below wooden floors is necessary.

Other construction issues that must be taken into consideration before the type of floor is decided are ventilation and insulation. Ventilation will deal with both the new floor and the existing, whereas insulation will be relevant to the new floor only.

UPGRADING THE EXISTING FLOOR

Where the existing garage floor is suitable for use within the new floor construction, then other factors will be involved in the upgrading process. For example, to prevent dampness rising through the ground and damaging the new floor, a damp-proof membrane will have to be installed. This membrane must span from wall to wall and provide a continuous barrier against rising damp.

Damp-proofing methods will be of particular interest and may come down to a selection from two possible methods. The first will be by way of a damp-proof membrane sheet onto which the finished or built-up floor is laid and the second may consist of a liquid membrane painted onto the existing concrete floor, also prior to the new floor being laid. This membrane is important in damp protection, so it must be installed correctly. The membrane sheeting can be laid over the base but precautions must be taken to reduce the risk of puncturing it and it must be dressed into the walls where the DPC is installed. Where a liquid membrane is used, this must be applied in full compliance with the manufacturer's recommendations. Short cuts at this stage are not recommended as they can lead to expensive repairs at a later date. When the selection of damp-proofing has been made and the membrane has been installed, then the building process will be carried out as described in the new floor construction process.

The hardcore base can be compacted using a mini-compactor hired from the local hire shop.

When the concrete floor is laid it must be tamped down and levelled off.

INSTALLING A NEW FLOOR

In many cases the existing garage floor will need to be removed completely and a new floor installed in its place. Where this is the case the approved building plans will detail the new floor construction where the following construction processes should be followed.

PREPARING THE OVERSITE

When the new external walls have been built up to DPC level or the existing walls have been readied for this next process, the area within these perimeter walls will be known as the oversite area. This oversite area may well consist simply of the existing garage floor base or it may include a new area if the existing garage is being extended. In any case this area must be stripped of all materials and, where weeds have grown through the floor, a good dose of weedkiller can be applied to prevent damage at a later date. Weeds have been known to grow through new floors where adequate precautions have not been taken. As well as weeds, all vegetation, vegetative materials and perishables such as wood or roots will have to be removed and the area completely cleared ready for the hardcore base to be laid. Again, and as a final precaution (and if you are in any doubt about the security of the floor and there is a slight risk that plants and the like may grow through the floor) spray the area again with a good weed-killer before starting the next stage.

When this oversite area has been prepared and levelled, an even bed of clean hardcore can be laid. The hardcore will need to be laid to a minimum depth of 150 mm and to a depth not greater than 300 mm, and should be layered where the floor area is deep. Old broken bricks and roof tiles often prove popular for this purpose but it is always wise to check with the building inspector about the suitability of any materials to be used. The best hardcore for this purpose will be of a manageable size and easy to consolidate without leaving unwanted air pockets. To create the best possible base for a solid floor the hardcore should be compacted using a heavy compactor or 'whacker plate' hired from the local plant hire centre.

At this stage, depending upon the type of floor insulation used, the floor insulation will be laid on top of the sand-blinded hardcore and beneath the damp-proof membrane sheeting. However, when you are laying a damp-proof membrane sheet on top of the hardcore and below the concrete oversite, then the hardcore must be 'blinded' with at least 12 mm of sharp sand to prevent the membrane being punctured by any sharp, hardcore projections.

Floor insulation can be installed below or above the damp-proof membrane.

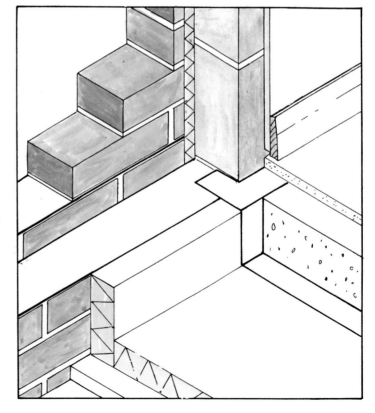

CONCRETE FLOOR INSULATION

Much is made of energy-saving in new homes and many of these rules make procedures subject to building regulations approval. With reference to the approved building plans the construction of the new floor will include specifications for this insulation in order to reduce any heat likely to be lost through the solid concrete floor. There are many proprietary methods available within building construction where all must meet the required 'U' values laid down in building regulations.

The layer of insulation, for solid concrete floors, will generally be laid on top of the compacted hardcore and prior to the damp-proof membrane and concrete oversite layer. This insulation layer is best laid below the membrane: it protects the membrane from puncture and remains stable during the pouring of the oversite concrete.

It is important to note that where polystyrene insulation sheets are used for floor insulation, they can be extremely difficult to manage when the oversite concrete is poured directly on top of them. They are liable to float, especially where the concrete is very wet, and it is difficult to prevent concrete seeping under the sheets. That is why it is best to put the membrane on top of the insulation before the concrete is added.

There are other variations of insulation for use under concrete flooring and if your approved plans specify a variation, this should be followed, though installation methods must be confirmed.

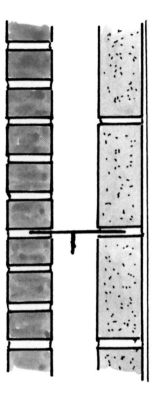

A cavity wall construction with properly installed wall tie.

DAMP-PROOF MEMBRANE

The damp-proof membrane will have to be installed to prevent damp rising through the concrete floor. The choice of membrane and the floor construction will be shown on the approved building plans and these should be followed. There are several different methods in operation to prevent dampness rising through the floor and these will vary, from membrane sheets laid on a sand-blinded bed through to a liquid bitumen painted or laid hot onto the concrete oversite.

The most popular choice will be the laying of a polythene film membrane sheet, of a quality applicable to the purpose, onto a sand-blinded base or directly onto the floor insulation. Where this is the choice you must make sure that where there are joins in the sheeting, they overlap adequately and are watertight. Also, extra care must be taken to remove the risk of puncturing the sheet before and during the process of laying it on the oversite area. Similar precautions must be taken when the concrete floor is poured onto it.

Second, a cold liquid bitumen, and there are several proprietary brands of solutions from which to choose, can be painted onto the oversite concrete and on the external walls, providing a continuous barrier with the DPC. When using these liquid bitumen barriers, the manufacturer's instructions must be followed carefully. In many cases, up to three coats will be required.

The third method of membrane is a hot bitumen, often called tanking, poured onto the primed oversite concrete area to a depth of not less than 3 mm. This method is often used in cellars to reduce damp coming through the walls and floor. Whichever method is chosen it is important to remember that the floor membrane must be dressed up to and join the existing and new DPCs to provide unbroken and continuous protection for the floor area.

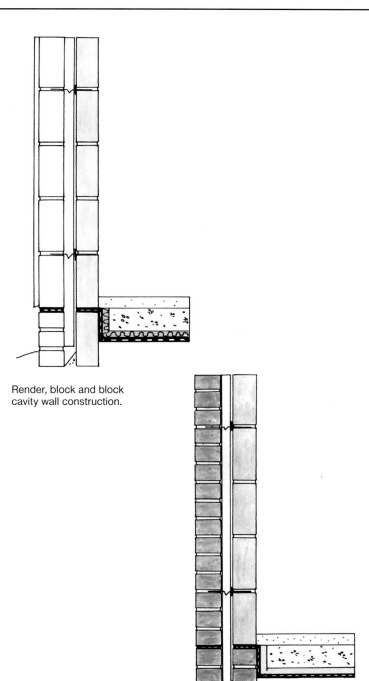

Render, block and block
cavity wall construction.

Brick and block
cavity construction.

Flooring

UNDERFLOOR VENTILATION

Underfloor ventilation must be addressed where new and existing timber floors form part of, or are adjacent to, the new refurbishment works.

To prevent dry rot and other airborne fungi causing damage to existing and new wooden floors, ventilation must be provided by way of a continuous flow of free air under suspended floors. More applicable for older properties where wooden floor joists and floorboards are common, and where the timbers are not or have not been treated against these perils, the existing airbricks providing an opening for this ventilation must be maintained. Where the air under the floor becomes stale and stagnant, in corners for example, there is always a risk that air conditions will become suitable for such unwanted attacks.

If you are installing a timber floor, always use timbers treated against such fungal and insect intrusions. Precautions must also be taken when building against walls where existing airbricks are positioned, to ensure that a free airflow to the floor in question is maintained. Where this occurs, new airbricks must be built into opposite external walls and, if the new floor is concrete, the air can be ducted into the area at risk by way of pipes laid under the oversite concrete.

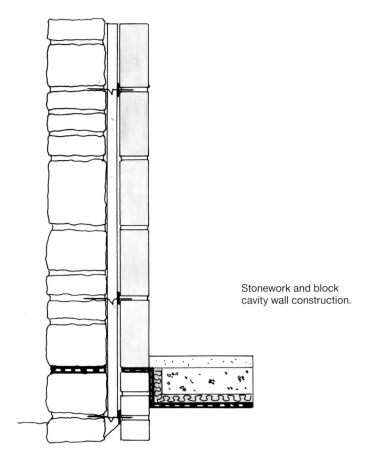

Stonework and block cavity wall construction.

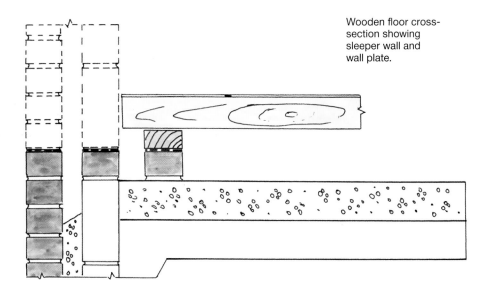

Wooden floor cross-section showing sleeper wall and wall plate.

Timber floor
section showing
herringbone struts.

AIRBRICKS

Where a proposed new solid concrete floor abuts an existing suspended wooden floor ,adequate underflow ventilation must be provided from new airbricks positioned in an external wall through ventilation pipes laid under the solid floor to the existing airbricks. Clay airbricks will be built into external walls up to 3 m apart and as far above ground level as possible but below damp-proof level. In corners where stagnant air can become a problem the airbricks will be situated within 450 mm of the corner. A purpose-made clay ducting is available to continue the ventilation through the inner wall and is built-in with the airbrick.

LAYERING THE OVERSITE CONCRETE

When the oversite area has been excavated, the hardcore has been laid, compacted and blinded with sand, the underfloor insulation has been installed and, if you are using a sheet damp-proof membrane, the membrane sheeting has been laid, then the next step is to pour the oversite concrete. Oversite concrete is commonly mixed at a 1:2:4 mix, which is slightly stronger than the foundation concrete that is commonly mixed at a ratio of 1:3:6.

As with the foundations, speed is the most important requirement when laying or pouring concrete. First mixing and then pouring the concrete should be a continuous process to ensure that each load bleeds in well with the previous load, maintaining the strength of the concrete. Do not pour in a load and then leave it for an hour or so before pouring in the next load. Concrete soon becomes dry and unworkable, forming a join where the two loads meet and this join is a weak point in the floor slab.

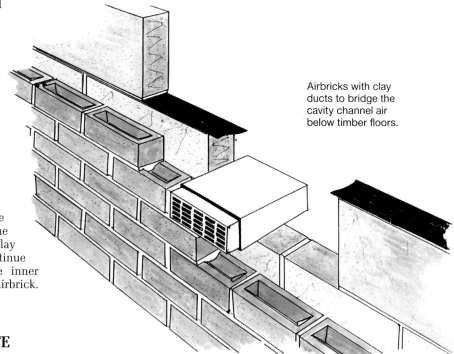

Airbricks with clay ducts to bridge the cavity channel air below timber floors.

When you are mixing the concrete by hand, at least one man should mix and pour while another levels off each load. For larger jobs pre-mixed concrete from a ready-mix supplier will save a lot of work and speed up the process. The concrete will be delivered to a mix you specify; 1:2:4 is most common for the oversite slab, and it is best ordered to a working consistency applicable to the circumstances.

If the concrete can be poured directly over the floor area all will be well but where the concrete has to be dumped onto a large plastic sheet and then 'barrowed' to the floor area ask the supplier about adding a retarder. This will give you a little 'working' time, usually a couple of hours, before the concrete starts to dry out.

Again, as with the foundation concrete, when you order concrete from a ready-mix supplier make sure you tell the supplier what the concrete is for. Tell them the size of the area being covered and the depth you are filling to. Also tell them if the load is to be dumped onto a sheet or poured directly into the new floor area. Do not calculate how much concrete is required to an exact amount; always allow a little extra for error.

Oversite concrete is generally laid to a minimum depth of 100 mm. If you are pouring the concrete onto a membrane the greatest care must be taken not to puncture it, which may result in problems at a later date. As the concrete is poured, it must be levelled and tamped down to remove air pockets, then left to cure for up to three days. Unlike the foundation concrete, it is unlikely to be exposed to excessive weather conditions, although the oversite concrete can still be vulnerable to frost and heat damage.

Of course, the best defence against frost damage is not to lay the concrete at all until the weather permits. If this is not possible, then it may be wise to cover the area with sacking or similar fibrous sheeting material, leaving a small gap between the concrete and the covering for airflow. If the weather is hot and sunny, the concrete drying out too quickly is the problem. For the best results the concrete must be kept damp for as long as possible, allowing curing to take place over two or three days. Shade from the sun is the best protection with constant, though not excessive, damping down to avoid fast drying out.

Beam and block floor with insulated chipboard flooring to finish.

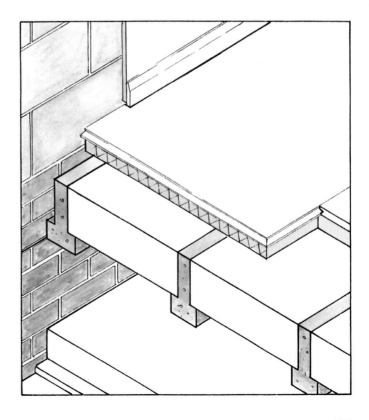

Where the oversite base is being reinforced, lay a half-layer of oversite concrete first, then lay on the reinforcing sheets, then pour on the top layer of concrete. Speed is important and a continuous flow must be achieved to allow the two layers to bleed together properly.

LEVELS

It is important during construction work that each section is laid properly. Overlooking the level of the hardcore or the insulation will have an effect on the level of the concrete, so try to get each level correct as the work progresses.

BEAM AND BLOCK FLOORS

Beam and block floors are becoming more and more common in domestic floor construction. This type of floor system works exceptionally well where the existing ground over which the new floor is being laid is either contaminated or needs building up. It is unlikely that contamination will be an issue where a garage floor is concerned, but raised levels may need to be addressed.

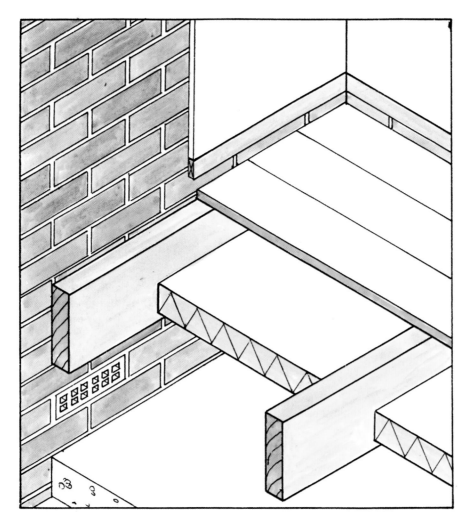

Fitting insulation and showing the position of airbricks in timber floor.

The construction of a beam and block floor is very straightforward. The precast concrete beams, reinforced with steel bars running through their length, will be installed to span the perimeter walls in the same way that timber joists span the floor area. The beams are manufactured off site. From the approved drawings the manufacturer will determine the length of each beam and produce a detailed drawing showing their finished position on site. Generally, the beams are positioned at centres to accommodate standard-size concrete wall blocks.

The one significant advantage the beam and block floors have over ground-supported concrete floors is that they save time: you do not have to wait for the floor to set. As soon as the beams are in place the concrete blocks can be laid, and a solid, secure base is immediately in place providing a secure working platform; this is certainly an advantage when compared with suspended timber floor construction.

Between the structural beams, aggregate or aircrete blocks can be laid to produce the solid floor base. It is on top of this base that the specified floor insulation will be laid prior to the approved finished floor surface.

A FLOATING FLOOR

The term 'floating floor' is often used to identify floors where the finished floor surface area is not secured – at least, not in a major way – to the floor base area. A floating floor can be a concrete screed, or it can be chipboard sheets. The construction methods are similar to ground-bearing concrete floors and suspended beam and block floors in that the base is a rigid one. A layer of rigid insulation, polystyrene or similar, is then added, with the finished floor surface laid on top of the insulation. This gives the impression of the surface 'floating' above the rigid concrete base.

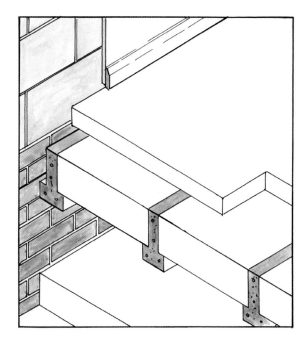

Beam and block flooring finished with sand and cement screed.

Beam and block flooring *in situ*.

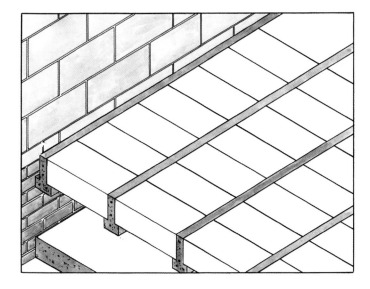

FLOOR SCREED

It is common in domestic building construction for solid floor construction to be finished off with a floor screed. This is a mixture of sand and cement laid to provide a flat, level and smooth finished surface. This method of construction – comprising a hardcore base, concrete slab, damp-proof membrane and finished off with a floor screed – has almost completely eliminated the risk of dry rot and other fungal damage previously attributed to timber floors. A layer of insulation can be installed between the concrete slab and the floor screed to ensure that it meets with building regulation requirements.

A floor screed is a mixture of sharp sand and cement in a ratio of between 1:3 and 1:4, depending on the depth of the screed. Where the floor is a floating floor the screed will be laid directly on top of the insulation. Where the screed is in excess of 50 mm, then you may consider a layer of wire mesh laid centrally within the screed to bind it together better. Discuss this possibility with the floor screeder before commencement.

Where there is underfloor heating incorporated into the floor screed, significant time must be allowed for the drying out process before the underfloor heating is used, to prevent abnormal shrinkage and cracking of the screed. This will also apply where a finished floor surface, including rigid floor tiles, is laid onto the screed floor.

UNDERFLOOR HEATING

This flooring section cannot be considered complete without consideration being given to underfloor heating. As the conversion is an addition to the existing dwelling, and therefore unlikely to be included in the existing heating layout, a simple addition by way of radiators may not be suitable for any number of reasons. These will include the location and size of the boiler, and location of existing pipework. Underfloor heating can therefore be viewed as a separate and alternative source, with possible financial savings in mind.

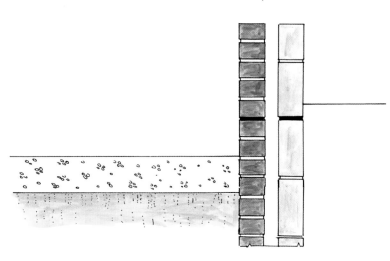

Existing concrete garage floor base laid directly on top of a compacted earth base.

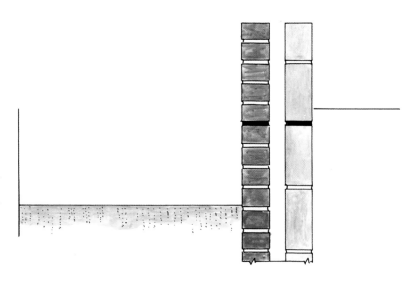

Remove existing garage floor and reduce base area to level required.

Underfloor heating is fast becoming the accepted form of heating for both domestic and commercial buildings, and is reputedly the simplest way to heat any room (large or small) evenly, efficiently and comfortably. Over the past decade, following in the footsteps of European designers and specifiers, the demand for underfloor heating has grown significantly, particularly in the colder northern countries where energy efficiency is vital. This is thanks partly to advances in modern technology and partly to the increased insulation of the modern home. This form of heating has prove to be energy-efficient, totally safe, silent and maintenance-free, and above all it creates the enviable situation where homeowners enjoy both greater comfort and lower fuel bills.

When you look at the issues of greater comfort and lower fuel bills individually, it is clear why demand is also growing from within the building construction industry. The first point, greater comfort, has been widely tested and it is clear that this is a heating system that is currently the best that modern science and technol-ogy can devise. The second point, lower fuel bills, is a result of energy efficiency within the building structure with results showing a clear saving when compared with other methods of heating. Underfloor heating is not new but with these clear advances in research, technology and home insulation it is fast becoming the heating system of the future.

Heating plays such a very important role in our daily lives because we spend more and more time indoors. For this reason the climate must be right even though it is created artificially and there-fore, for it to work properly, it must also be supported with adequate and suit-able ventilation in and around our living areas.

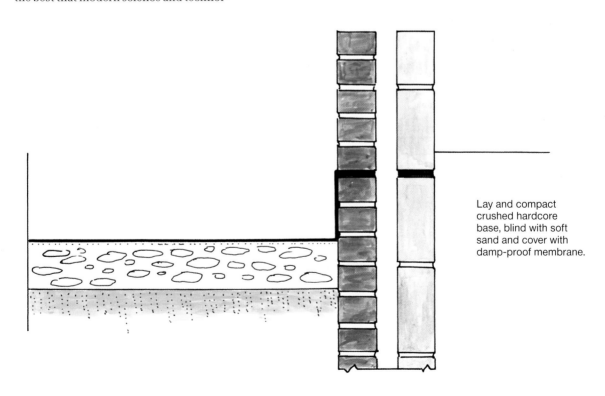

Lay and compact crushed hardcore base, blind with soft sand and cover with damp-proof membrane.

Flooring

Designing an underfloor heating system will involve several factors including wall construction, ceiling heights, glazing, insulation and, of course, the proposed floor covering. The system can be installed at ground-floor level and also at first-floor level where all rooms, and in particular the tiled floors of kitchens and bathrooms, will benefit greatly from this heat source.

Of course, the main principle of underfloor heating is not new and it is based on the simple fact that warm air rises. When this is compared directly with a central heating system designed principally around radiators (where the heat starts to rise some way from the floor creating a ceiling temperature significantly higher than the floor temperature) this form of heating has clear advantages. A significant point is that underfloor heating is invisible, allowing complete freedom of interior design, maximizing wall space and allowing furniture to be placed where it looks and functions best. It ensures that there are no cold corners, draughts or cold floors and, as ideal comfort conditions require, your feet are a few degrees warmer than your head. The entire floor is heated, and warmth is radiated evenly and gently. The task of decorating will be greatly reduced with no more radiators to paint. A further significant point is that there are very few restrictions on floor coverings: warm tiled floors in kitchens and bathrooms, and warm wooden and carpeted floors all affect the whole ambience of the room and help to create a very pleasant comfort level.

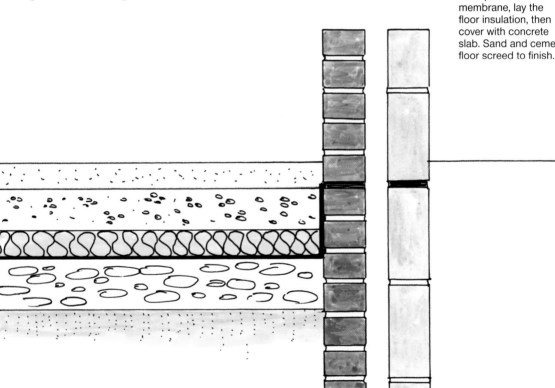

On top of the membrane, lay the floor insulation, then cover with concrete slab. Sand and cement floor screed to finish.

Ensure the correct depth of insulation is installed.

The floor surface temperature used in underfloor heating applications is generally between 25 °C and 27 °C. This is lower than the body temperature and, unlike wall-hung radiators, eliminates the risk of burns to children and the elderly. The heat transfer with this type of system is mainly radiant and therefore it does not rely on air movement. This minimizes the circulation of airborne dust and lowers the likelihood of allergic respiratory reactions.

On a practical point there are currently two significant forms of underfloor heating: the first is electrical and the second is a hot water system. Both can be used with most types of floor finish or covering and, of course, both are totally invisible. The electrical system is a series of thin profile, double-insulated cables attached to an open weave mat. The system complies with all the current electrical safety requirements, even allowing for use in wet areas such as bathrooms and kitchens. The cables are positioned at specific 'centres', ensuring an even heat distribution with the matting silently warming the surface of the floor to an even temperature. This type of heating is easy to install on any solid-based and level floor prior to laying the floor covering.

Pipes buried in the concrete base should be set approx. 38 mm from perimeter walls, in a 150 mm-wide channel and should be approx. 38 mm deep.

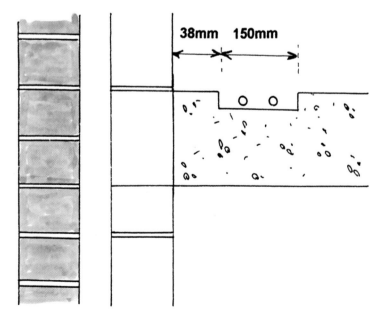

38mm   150mm

Flooring

The warm water-based system is formulated from a continuous run of polyethylene-type tubing and there are several methods of installation, though the heating system must be positioned above the layer of floor insulation. At first-floor level, and perhaps in floating floors, the pipes are laid on aluminium diffusion plates to prevent downward heat transmission. These plates also help to spread the heat. The heating pipes are designed to be resistant to limescale build up and the normal levels of chlorine found in the domestic water system. When the pipes and plates are in place the floor covering can then be laid. The maintenance of an underfloor system is likely to be minimal because the heating element will not corrode or scale.

The benefits of this type of heating system are clear and installation in new buildings is increasing as greater awareness of the advantages become known. In most of the countries of mainland Europe, and in particular where insulation requirements are higher than the UK, underfloor heating has already become the preferred form of domestic central heating.

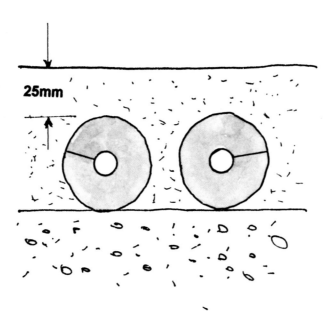

25mm

A good covering of screed above pipes is required.

STEP-BY-STEP SUMMARY

1. Where the existing garage floor is not good enough to upgrade, excavate fully to a suitable depth for the new floor.
2. When the area is excavated, lay a good layer of crushed stone or clean hardcore, blinded with sand for a smooth surface.
3. Where applicable, lay the rigid insulation on top of the sand-blinded hardcore base.
4. Where a damp-proof membrane is being installed lay it on top of the rigid insulation making sure not to puncture the surface.
5. With the membrane in place the concrete base can be laid, taking extra care not to puncture the polythene membrane.
6. The floor screed can be laid directly on top of the concrete base to finish off.

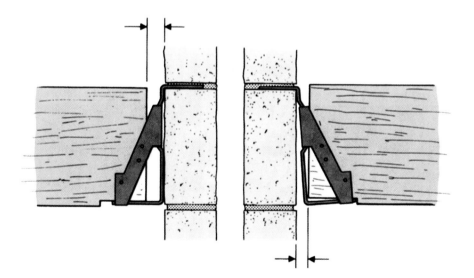

Incorrect joist hanger connections.

> **POINT OF GOOD BUILDING PRACTICE 8**
> Where floor and roofing joists are supported by joist hangers make sure they are installed correctly. The joist hanger must fit tightly against the wall and the joist must be secured into the hanger with a gap of 10mm maximum, to allow for expansion.

TIMBER FLOORING

With garage conversion work, or in fact any conversion work involving existing old floors, the installation of a suspended floor may well make a lot of sense, save time and hugely reduce the work involved with excavations and so on. By simply suspending the timbers above the existing garage floor area a solid floor can be obtained fairly quickly and with excellent results. However, there are strict guidelines to be followed and an installation process that must meet with the existing guidelines of good building practice.

SUSPENDED TIMBER FLOORS

Where a timber floor is constructed at ground-floor level it is called a 'suspended' floor, and where a timber floor is constructed at first-floor level it is referred to as a 'single' or 'upper' floor.

Building up to or adjoining an existing timber floor in an existing dwelling will require just as much attention to the specifics as would be involved with a new concrete floor. Insulation and ventilation are prime areas that attract close attention from the Building Control Department and each new floor must meet their strict criteria.

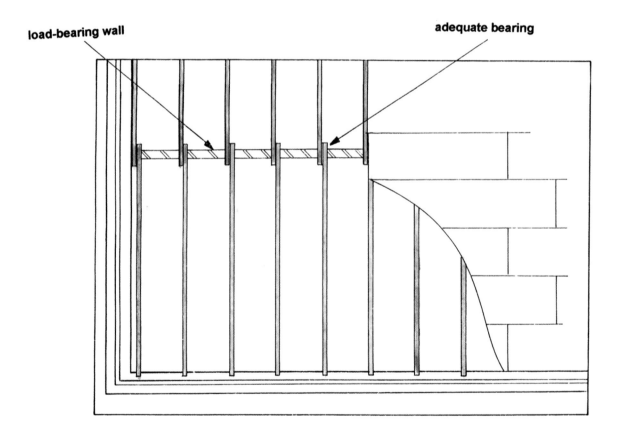

load-bearing wall

adequate bearing

Floor joists resting on a sleeper or supporting wall.

112

A 'suspended' floor can provide a perfect explanation for floors built in this way. The floor timbers will be suspended above the concrete oversite, resting on and built into the perimeter walls. In many cases the walls will be close enough together for the new timbers to span the distance without additional support being required. Where this is not the case or where there is a limited depth for the timbers to be installed, then sleeper walls will be required. A sleeper wall is built in brick and can be as low as one brick high with a wall plate bedded on top for the joists to rest on. Where the sleeper walls exceed one brick in height, then the walls will be built in a kind of honeycomb design to allow for 'free air' ventilation to work properly under the floor area.

To assist this free passage of air under a suspended floor, airbricks will need to be built into the external walls of the building at approximately 650 mm centres. The top of the sleeper wall should be level with the DPC. To reduce the risk of damp problems the flooring timbers will not be built into the external walls below either the DPC or ground level.

The floor joists for suspended floors can vary in size and can even be as small as 100 mm × 50 mm on a 100 mm × 50 mm wall plate with the underfloor insulation fitted under and between the joists. Any variations in joist size and the centres at which the joists need to be set will be specified clearly on your approved building plans and may vary relative to the span between supporting walls.

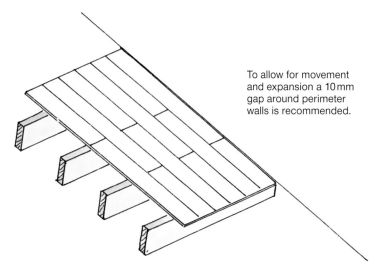

To allow for movement and expansion a 10 mm gap around perimeter walls is recommended.

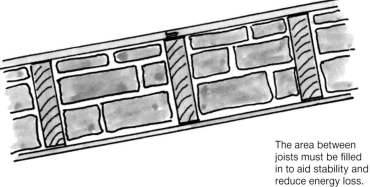

The area between joists must be filled in to aid stability and reduce energy loss.

Timber Flooring

SETTING OUT THE NEW FLOOR JOISTS

Your approved building plans will show the positioning and the expected spans of the new joists. The timbers should be ordered to achieve this span but cut to size according to the site measurements and not according to the plan measurements, in case they differ slightly. Where a joist is expected to span from one wall to an opposite supporting wall, always allow for the joist to pass over the wall completely, do not cut it short. The calculations made will allow for the joist to rest on the full width of the supporting wall. An overhang will not be necessary.

When the joists are installed they will need to be levelled off before a floor covering is fitted. For the professional, 'eyeing' them in is as good a method as any. They line up the top of the joists by eye to tell whether or not all the joist tops are in line. A more accurate method could be to use a straight edge and a spirit level. Where a joist is out of line, packing may be required. When a joist is badly bowed causing the levels to fluctuate, a replacement joist may be the best solution.

HERRINGBONE STRUTS/NOGGINS

To stabilize the timber joists, for both a flat roof and a floor, a row of herringbone struts or noggins will need to be installed midway along the length of the joist. If,

however, the span exceeds 4m, then two rows of struts may be required. The struts can be cut from timber or they can be bought from the supplier and securely nailed in place. Noggins must be at least half the depth of the joists in question, so where the joists are 200mm deep the noggin should be at least 100mm deep.

Where the joist run ends adjacent to a wall, for example, timber wedges can be installed to provide an overall and continuous rigidity to the whole floor.

'Catnic' herringone struts.

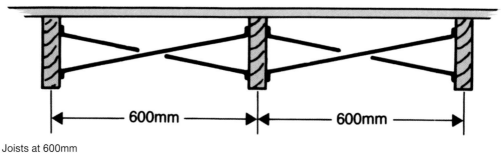

Joists at 600mm centres with herringbone struts.

DOUBLE JOISTS

Where additional loading is expected, over and above the load calculated for the new joists, it may be necessary to double up the new joists. This is more likely where additional lightweight or studwork walls are to be built. Double and even triple joists are regularly specified in order to reduce the necessity for foundation work.

CABLES AND PIPES

Apart from the relocation of existing cables and water pipes to accommodate the new joists, there is the addition of new fittings for the new rooms to consider. The intended position of electric light fittings and power points must be clearly marked and the cables must be installed prior to laying the floor covering (or the fixing of ceilings). Water pipes for radiators and other plumbing fittings must also be in place along with any drainage pipes required to dispose of foul waste from a toilet, or water from a bath or shower. These fittings must be positioned correctly, attached to and passed through the new joists safely, and their positions should be highlighted to avoid damage when the floor and ceiling coverings are fitted.

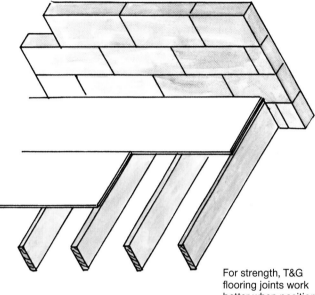

For strength, T&G flooring joints work better when positioned directly above a joist. Where this is not possible, noggins will be required.

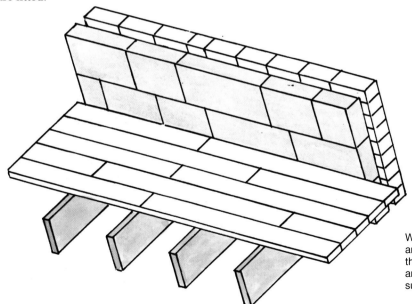

Where floorboards are butted together the joins must be arranged over supporting floor joists.

FLOOR COVERING

The finished floor surface can be sheet decking or floorboards. The boarding must be secured to the joists to achieve the best results. To prevent floors from squeaking and cracking when in use, first apply a suitable wood glue to the joists, according to the manufacturer's instructions, and then secure the boards in place using self-tapping screws.

The floor covering will usually be a choice of timber floorboards or sheet coverings of chipboard or plywood. Softwood floorboards are available with a tongued and grooved (T&G) finish for strength, in a variety of widths up to 150mm. Similarly, the sheet coverings are available in a variety of sizes, though only the chipboard sheeting is likely to be available with a T&G finish. The floor coverings should be secured at right angles to the joists.

Where the sheets do not meet directly over a supporting joist, a noggin should be added to provide additional support. Chipboard flooring is very common and is widely used in the modern housebuilding industry. It is available in a variety of grades and a large area can be covered easily in a very quick time. Be sure to specify flooring-grade chipboard; it has extra water resistance and is more suitable for flooring than standard chipboard sheeting.

FLOOR INSULATION

Insulation will be required in the new floor and is available in a variety of types and sizes. There is mineral wool insulation and rigid board insulation, for example. With energy conservation playing such a huge role in home design, new floors in particular attract the closest inspection. The installation of insulation will have a two-pronged effect. First, it will retain heat within the building and second, it will help to restrict noise from either leaving or entering the building.

There are a great many ways of reducing noise through floor areas but they all require installation before the decking is laid rather than a later stage, so consideration must be given at an early stage. Insulation in the floor void will act as a partial sound barrier but close attention must also be given to the floor covering.

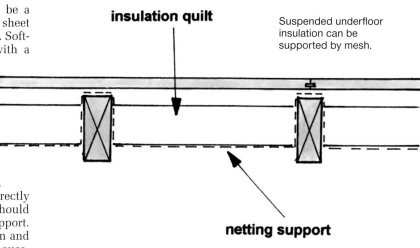

insulation quilt

Suspended underfloor insulation can be supported by mesh.

netting support

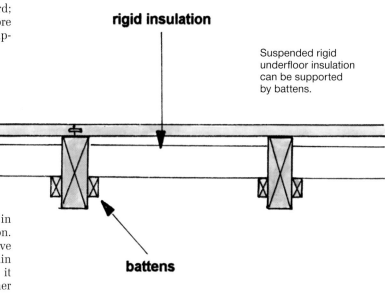

rigid insulation

Suspended rigid underfloor insulation can be supported by battens.

battens

One of the many methods devised in recent years is the fitting of sound-deadening strips to the top of the floor joists before the floor covering is laid. Another is the fixing of upgraded, sound-insulated chipboard sheeting, made especially for this purpose. Taking extra care in this area will reap huge rewards when the work is completed, and even more so when the new rooms are to be used by children or teenagers.

A note of caution here. When adding insulation strips, upgraded chipboard or insulated floor coverings, make sure that the extra floor dimensions are included in the building plans, otherwise you may find that the ceiling levels are lower than anticipated and the fitting of doors into existing frames will prove difficult.

GARAGE ROOF SPACE

Where the roof space in the garage is also to be converted into living space, then the original ceiling joists will become floor joists. To achieve this, structural questions will need to be satisfied. Will the existing roof and in particular the joists, which were originally designed to carry 'dead' loads, be suitable to carry 'live' loads?

In simple terms a 'dead' load is the weight of materials used to construct the roof and a 'live' load is the combination of the dead load plus people and furniture.

For domestic dwellings, and in particular for conversion work, building regulations have determined a loading table so that new floor joists can be calculated in kilograms per square metre. To ensure that the new joists can carry the load to be imposed upon them (and this will inevitably determine the size of the new joists) you will first need to know the maximum span, or distance between load-bearing supports, that the joists will be required to cover. With this measurement you can refer to the tables that will list the joists by strength or grade, dimension and centre, or how far the joists should be spaced apart.

Calculating first-floor joist sizes need not be complicated but the whole of the roof dynamics will be changed when the roof area is also to be converted. In this instance a structural engineer will provide the best joist size and centre, and indicate what other structural work is required to retain the integrity of the new roof.

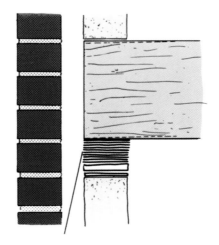

Packing must be of non-compressible materials.

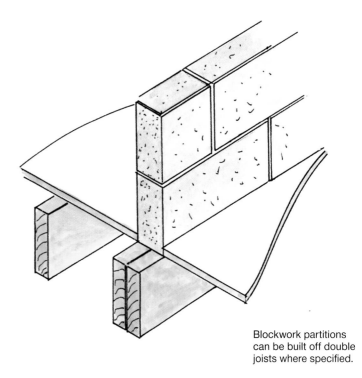

Blockwork partitions can be built off double joists where specified.

Timber Flooring

STEP-BY-STEP SUMMARY

1. A suspended wooden floor may prove to be the best solution and help to avoid excavating the existing garage floor.
2. The new floor joists should rest fully on the supporting perimeter walls.
3. For added stability a row of herringbone struts or noggins will be installed.
4. Once the joists are stable any cables and pipes to go under the floor can then be installed.
5. Floor insulation will have a dual role in retaining heat and reducing noise.
6. For best results the floor covering will first be glued, then screwed to the new joists.

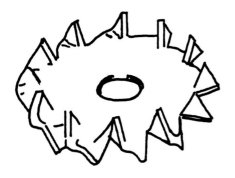

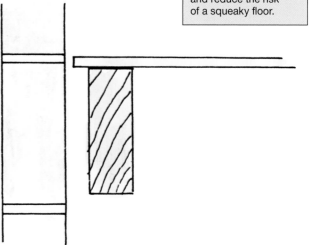

> **POINT OF GOOD BUILDING PRACTICE 9**
> Always allow a 10mm gap around perimeter walls where wooden flooring is being installed. This will allow for any expansion and reduce the risk of a squeaky floor.

ROOFING

Garage conversions will vary in size, design and application and many will not require or involve significant alterations to the existing main roof structure, especially where the garage is adjoined to a modern dwelling. However, where the garage is being built over, forming a second storey requiring the roof structure to be removed or where the roof structure is simply not suitable for direct conversion for domestic purposes and cannot be upgraded, then a complete removal and rebuild may be the only answer.

Covering all the possibilities will not be possible but the construction will remain the same with conversion work as with any other development and must meet the necessary building requirements for new roofs.

Existing structures can be upgraded to comply with current building regulations with the minimum of fuss or disruption and the approved building plans must clearly specify existing and new works. The structure will only be approved if it meets with the current building requirements.

Where the conversion work necessitates a new roof, then the choice will be either a flat roof or a pitched roof. The decision must not be made lightly and long-term plans must be taken into consideration. On the upside, a flat roof is likely to be less expensive to construct than a pitched roof. On the downside, a flat roof does suffer from a limited lifetime and it can also be less visually appealing than a pitched roof. Inevitably, the choice of roof construction will affect the time frame but with a small project such as a garage conversion, the effect will not be as great as if it were a larger construction.

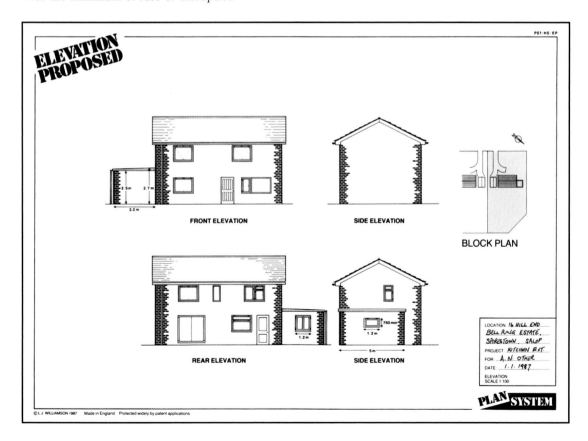

119

Roofing

CHOICE 1: THE FLAT ROOF

The flat roof has, historically, been widely used in the Middle East for many centuries where the climate is dry and arid, but it wasn't until the nineteenth century and the introduction of a gradual improvement of waterproofing techniques that the flat roof became more and more widely used in Europe.

Possibly the simplest of all roofs to install, the flat roof has become extremely popular on single-storey buildings, extensions and conversions, though in more recent years building control and planning departments have been reluctant to allow their use on buildings above one storey.

In construction a flat roof consists of timber joists resting on and secured to wall plates. Decking sheets are then secured to the joists prior to layers of bitumen felt being built up and laid hot onto the sheets. It is the layers of hot bitumen and special roofing felt that provide the important waterproof covering. Insulation for the roof structure can be laid on top of the joists or between them to ensure that the structure achieves the energy-saving requirements necessary to comply with building regulations.

It is the location of this insulation that differentiates the two roof types. The first is known as a cold roof and the second is known as a warm roof. The cold roof is constructed with the insulation fitted in the roof void, between the roof decking and the ceiling boards. To prevent condensation problems occurring in cold roofs, the void, the area in the roof space between the joists, must be ventilated to allow clear air to flow above the insulation and below the roof deck. This clear airflow will be assisted by ventilation gaps along the sides of the roof. The warm roof is constructed with the insulation built in-between the bitumen felt waterproof covering and the flat roof decking. A vapour barrier is fitted between these two layers.

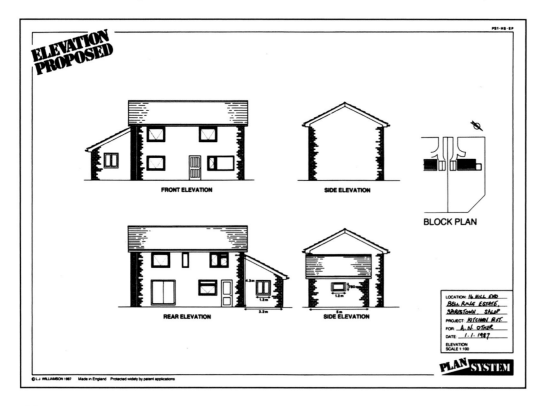

FLAT ROOF CONSTRUCTION

To construct a flat roof, timber joists will be installed spanning from one wall to an opposite wall. They will be laid level and at agreed centres (as shown on the approved building plans), ready for the flat-roof decking to be attached. When ordering roof joists there are three factors to consider.

Factor one is size. The joist sizes are likely to be 150 mm × 50 mm, 175 mm × 50 mm and 200 mm × 50 mm. These are the most common sizes in use today but the size for each construction will differ owing to any number of circumstances. The timber sizes will be specified on the plans.

Factor two is grade. Timber is graded by its strength and the grade for each construction will also be specified on the building plans. There are three common grades of timber in use for this type of construction. They are general stress (GS) grade, special stress (SS) grade and machine general stress (MGS) grade. The GS and SS grades are assessed visually, noting the grain and the position of knots in the timber and so on, and the MGS grade is assessed mechanically.

Factor three is length. The length of the joists may be calculated from the plans but will be better calculated from the building itself, allowing a little extra length for tolerances and for installation.

Each joist will be fitted to the wall plate at a specified 'centre' as shown on the plans. The 'centre' measurement is taken from the centre of one joist to the centre of the adjacent joists, and so on. You may reduce the centres, to accommodate the decking sheets for example, but you should not increase the centres without prior discussion with the building inspector. The joist sizes will be calculated by the length of span, from one wall to another, and the load imposed upon them (in this case the felt roof). When the joists are in position and firmly nailed to the wall plate, mild steel restraint straps will be fitted, securing the wall plate to the wall. The restraint straps should be fitted at approximately 2 m centres, starting within 450 mm of any corners. They will be securely fixed to a joist and will extend down the wall at least 1 m. These straps will then be secured firmly to the wall with at least four fixings – galvanized nails or screws are recommended – with the lowest fixing no more than 150 mm from the bottom.

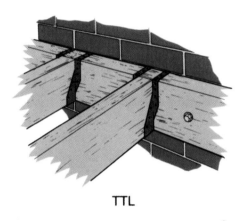

TTL

'Catnic' joist hangers.

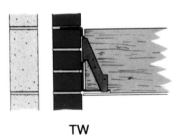

TW

CONDENSATION

Another area of concern that is treated with suitable respect by the building regulations is condensation in the roof void. Condensation is formed where hot air meets cooler air, and the roof void is a prime example. Large quantities of condensation are produced in the average modern home from activities such as cooking, taking a bath and having a shower. Even breathing and perspiring produces condensation. This warm, moist air will be drawn by convection to parts of the building where the air is cooler. Modern homes are now so very well insulated in the walls and windows that the roof void can be a very vulnerable area if it is not insulated and ventilated properly. Once the warm air has entered the roof void, condensation can occur. To prevent this becoming a problem, cross ventilation must be designed to ensure a free passage of air in this area. This passage of free air will help to remove the warm air before damaging condensation can occur.

CROSS-VENTILATION

A great deal of condensation is generated within the modern home, often forming in roof spaces where cold air meets and warm air. In order to reduce the risk of condensation damage to roof timbers and fixings, and to prevent mould growth, an effective roof ventilation system will be required.

Cross-ventilation will be effective where free air is allowed to flow from one side of the roof to the other without interruption above the layer of insulation and below the flat-roof decking. To achieve this a gap at least 50 mm wide should be left between the roof insulation and the roof decking. This will provide a good space for ventilation over the bulk of the roof, supported by continuous ventilation along the eaves. This continuous ventilation will be provided by openings along opposite sides of the roof. The openings can be a continuous gap along the eaves where eaves ventilators can be fitted or alternatively circular eaves ventilators can be fixed into the soffit board [see illustration].

Whichever system you choose, the combined areas of the opening must be equivalent to a continuous gap of 25 mm running the full length of the eaves. Where the openings run in the same direction as the roof joists, notches can be cut into the firring pieces [see below] at regular intervals to aid cross-ventilation.

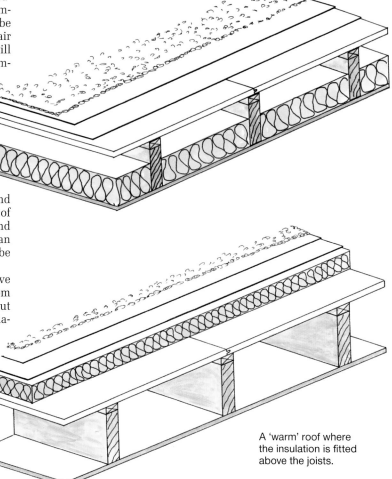

A 'cold' roof where the insulation is fitted between the joists.

A 'warm' roof where the insulation is fitted above the joists.

Flat roof detail.

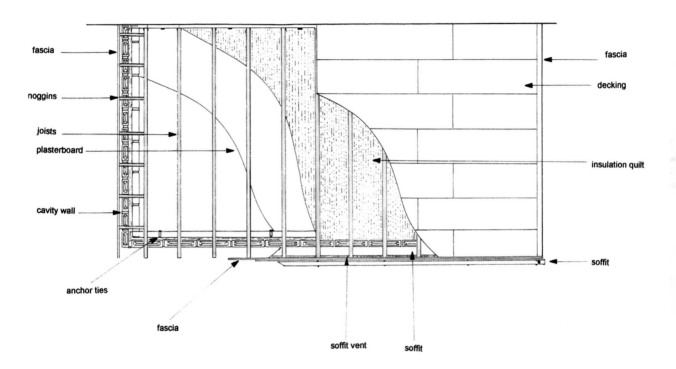

fascia

fascia

noggins

decking

joists

plasterboard

insulation quilt

cavity wall

soffit

anchor ties

fascia

soffit vent

soffit

SETTING OUT THE FLAT-ROOF JOISTS

When the wall plate is securely fixed, the flat-roof joists can be fitted. Working with the decking sheets in mind, the joists should be positioned to ensure minimum wastage. To produce a secure and stable structure it is advisable to ensure that the decking sheets join on a joist. This will help to strengthen the deck and also reduce wastage. Install the first joist close to the wall and work from this, ensuring the joist centres do not exceed those specified on the building plans. You will then find that the ceiling boards will also fit nicely if the joists are properly positioned, also reducing wastage.

THE 'FIRRING' SECTION

The term 'a flat roof' is slightly misleading because, in fact, the roof is not really flat. If the roof were flat then the dispersal of rainwater would prove difficult and the effect of water laying on the roof for long periods of time may well increase the risk of water penetration and is likely to reduce the life of the flat roof substantially. To provide the necessary slope on a flat roof, and to direct the rainwater away and into the guttering, a piece of timber commonly known as a firring piece will be fitted to each joist before the decking is laid. A firring piece is a strip of timber already machine-cut by your supplier. It will be the same width as the joist, and, when secured to the joist, will provide a fall or slope of at least 1 in 40. This is the required slope, according to building regulations, for draining water off the roof area.

DECKING

When the roof joists and firring pieces are in place and secure, then the sheets of decking can be fitted. There will be a choice of materials for the decking and this will include sheets of exterior-grade plywood or T&G chipboard to provide a stable 'deck' onto which the hot bitumen felt or (if you are building a warm roof) the insulation can be laid. The materials most suitable for this purpose will be specified on the approved building plans. With the roof joists centred to reduce wastage and to provide support for the sheets where joins occur, the decking can be nailed to the roof joists using galvanized nails. The thickness of the plywood or chipboard sheets you use will be specified on the building plans and will be determined by the space between the joists.

Where insulation is fitted between the joists, adequate space must be left to allow free air movement above the insulation.

Insulation quilt and ventilation.

TILT FILLET

A tilt fillet is a triangular-shaped piece of timber used around the perimeters of flat roofs to provide a guide for deflecting rainwater into the gutters. The tilt fillet will be nailed to the decking, along the edges where required. The bitumen felt roofing, finished in a layer of mineral felt, will be dressed over it for protection.

FELT ROOFING

Asphalt, bitumen-based waterproofing methods have been in use for many centuries and records can be found as far back as the rebuilding of Babylon and more recently (well, at least 200 years ago) this material was applied to ships' timbers to make them waterproof and more seaworthy. A natural product, asphalt can be produced from limestone rocks and shale, and in some areas is found in a liquid form. This natural asphalt is not found in the UK but is common in France, Switzerland and Germany where asphalt-impregnated limestone is mined. The largest natural, liquid-form asphalt deposit can be found in Trinidad, known as Trinidad Asphalt Lake, and it has a consistency almost dense enough to walk on.

Recent years have seen great improvements in the durability of asphalt, resulting in widespread usage throughout the building industry. Mastic asphalt and bitumen-based roofing felt have been combined to produce a highly efficient and commonly used waterproof membrane for flat roofs in particular.

The built-up bitumen roof, the most popular form of multi-layer roofing, has gone through rigorous testing over recent years. As a result of this extensive testing, in the UK a British Standard CP 144 Part 4, covering the application of mastic asphalt roofing, and BS 747, covering bitumen-based roofing felt, are being enforced. There are two forms of built-up roof: the first is used on cold roofs and the second on warm roofs. When applying a built-up bitumen roof-covering to a cold roof, the first layer of felt is secured to the deck, using hot bitumen or large-headed galvanized nails followed by at least two layers of felt bonded in hot bitumen. Importantly, the additional layers must have staggered joints with an overlap of at least 50 mm where joints occur.

The tilt fillet timber strip is designed to direct rainwater towards the guttering.

Joists should not overlap more than 100mm.

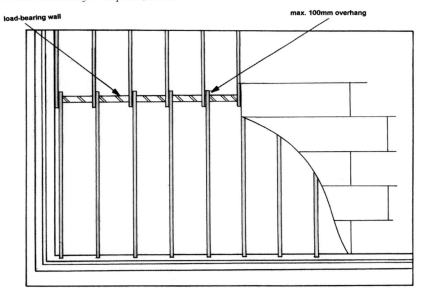

load-bearing wall · max. 100mm overhang

Roofing

To finish off a layer of reflective mineral felt will be fitted to exposed areas and a layer of reflective stone chippings will be bedded in bitumen to protect the roof from the effects of ultraviolet radiation.

For a warm roof the waterproof covering is laid on top of the insulation, but first a vapour barrier must be bedded on top of the decking, on top of which the insulation is to be laid. A perforated layer of felt is then laid on top of the insulation with hot bitumen poured over the top, sealing it to the insulation through the perforations. A top layer, as with the cold roof, is bedded on and then the process is finished in the same way as for a cold roof. It is important to avoid walking (or any traffic movement at all) on the completed roof as this can cause punctures, resulting eventually in a breakdown of the waterproof membrane.

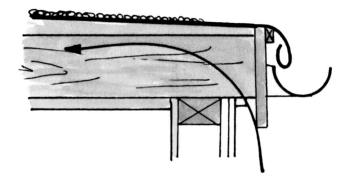

Access for air to ventilate the roof space will be required.

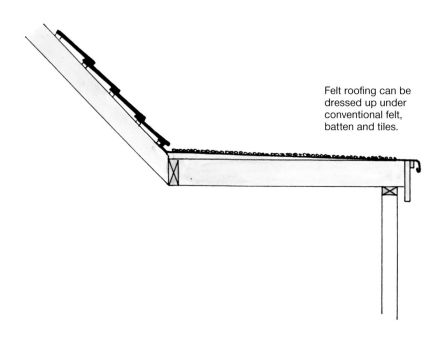

Felt roofing can be dressed up under conventional felt, batten and tiles.

CHOICE 2: THE PITCHED OR SLOPING ROOF

Roof coverings have changed very little during the last 1,000 years. Ever since mankind left his cave and lived in the portable structures commonly seen in use in some parts of Africa, simple roof coverings became essential. A sloping roof made from branches covered with dead plants and grasses progressed into the thatched roof we know and love today. Handmade clay tiles, dating as far back as the thirteenth century, were used to cover roofs in areas where suitable clay was found, eventually replacing the thatched roof as the number-one roof covering. Clay tiles, now made by machine, can be seen in numerous shapes, sizes and colours throughout the country.

The roof structure, flat or pitched, has also progressed with a mass of regulations to ensure that it is strong enough to carry the load imposed upon it, that it is insulated to assist energy conservation and ventilated sufficiently to prevent condensation damage. Add to this the roof's appearance and how it compares with the existing building and you will realize how multi-functional a roof is now designed to be.

PITCHED ROOF CONSTRUCTION

A roof is classified as a pitched roof when the pitch or slope exceeds 10 degrees, though acceptable roof coverings for domestic extensions and conversions, such as tiles and slates, dictate that the slope should be in excess of 17.5 degrees to provide the required protection from water penetration.

A pitched roof is a construction configured with rafters and ceiling joists, where lean-to roofs, close-coupled roofs and the less popular mono-pitched roof will cover the majority of choices. There are two recommended ways of building a pitched roof.

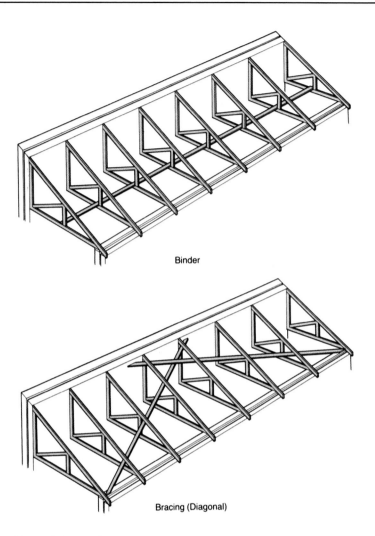

Binder

Bracing (Diagonal)

Mono-pitched roofs.

The first and most common construction for conversion work is a 'cut' roof. This is a pitched roof formed by the carpenter, on site, from timbers cut to length to form rafters and joists. The timber dimensions will be specified on your plans but the timber lengths will not be, so leave the ordering to the carpenter who will make allowances for angles and overhangs.

The second choice of roof construction is the use of truss rafters. A truss rafter is a machine-made roof member of rafters and ceiling joists. It is structurally designed and made to suit your particular individual requirements. Truss rafters are often much easier to install than a 'cut' roof, reducing labour costs significantly, but the material costs can be notably higher for these smaller projects where only a few trusses are involved. Even so, you may want to weigh up the total cost of a 'cut' roof, including labour, in order to compare it with the cost of a truss roof, including labour. Your local supplier will provide you with a quotation for the trusses and the carpenter will quote you for the labour. Whichever roof structure you choose, when the timbers or the trusses arrive on site they must be stored on a flat and level surface in a dry place until they are required for use.

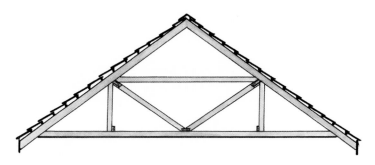

also secure the two together but do not connect them along the length of the timbers. New joists and ceiling joists are best kept apart, thus reducing damage to the existing ceiling below caused by hammering or any other general movement.

Duo-pitched
roofs.

SETTING OUT THE CEILING JOISTS

Your approved building plans will show the positioning and the expected spans of the new joists and they should be cut to length accordingly. When a joist is to span from the eaves to a supporting wall, always allow for the joist to pass over the wall completely. An overhang of, say, 50–80 mm will be sufficient, ensuring that the whole of the wall is supporting the joist. At the eaves the joist can be cut at the same angle as the roof, making it easier to slide into place, resting on the wall plate. At this point in the eaves, where the joist abuts an existing rafter, the two can be securely attached to each other. Where the joist abuts a ceiling joist at the eaves you can

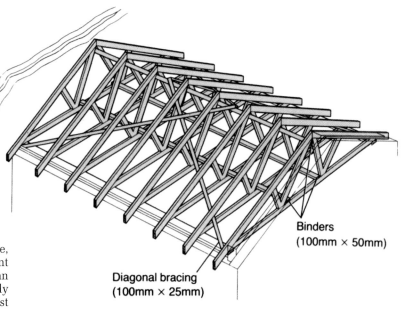

Binders
(100mm × 50mm)

Diagonal bracing
(100mm × 25mm)

In the majority of cases keeping the joists independent of the existing ceiling structure is advisable. Where the joists rest on supporting walls a small, 2 mm packing can be inserted, removing the possibility of damage to lower floor ceilings necessitating expensive repairs or even replacement.

When the joists are installed they will need to be levelled off, as with the floor joists described in Chapter 9. For the professional, 'eyeing' them in is as good a method as any. They line up the top of the joists by eye to tell whether or not all the joist tops are in line. A more accurate method could be to use a straight edge and a spirit level. Where joists are out of line, packing may be needed. When a joist is badly bowed causing the levels to fluctuate, a replacement may be required.

Allow sufficient overhang for fascia and soffits where required.

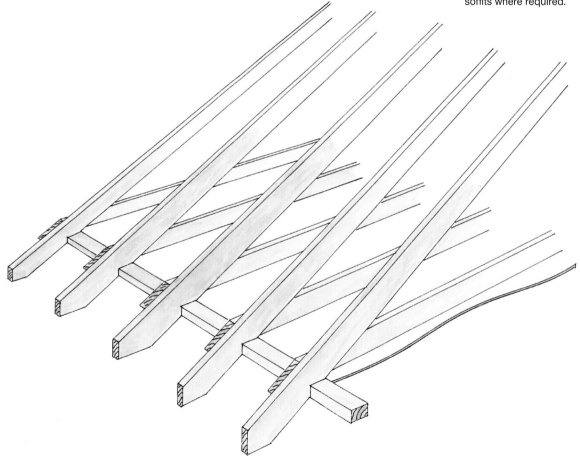

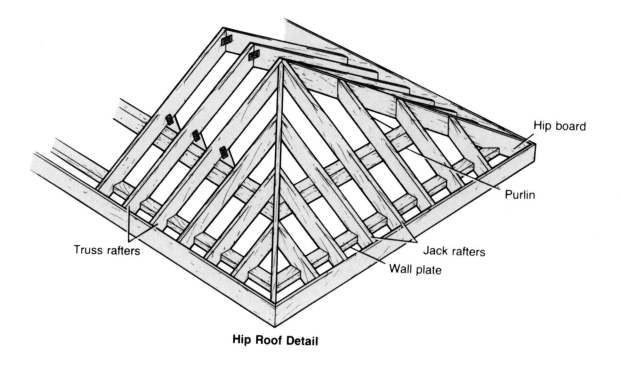

Hip board

Purlin

Truss rafters

Jack rafters

Wall plate

Hip Roof Detail

LEAN-TO ROOF

A lean-to roof has a single slope, generally away from the existing building and secured to a wallplate at both ends. The rafters may be supported mid-span depending upon the distance between the walls and the weight of the roof covering. A lean-to roof can be built with a slope as low as 17.5 degrees where it will be covered with large interlocking concrete tiles manufactured for this purpose. The shallower the slope, the more tile overlap is required.

CLOSE-COUPLED ROOF

A close-coupled roof has a double pitch where two rafters are fixed to a central ridge board at one end and to the wall plates, on opposite walls, at the other. A ceiling joist will then span from wall plate to wall plate and will be secured to the rafters to prevent them from spreading apart. Larger variations of a close-coupled roof may well require additional support built into the structure, such as purlins and struts. The purlins, where

specified, will be positioned midway along the rafters. This added support will help to increase the span of the rafters without having to increase the timber size. The timber struts will be positioned to assist in this load-bearing exercise and will, where possible, direct the roof load down to a load-bearing point such as an internal wall structure. As further structural support and to maintain the integrity of the roof, binders and hangers will provide increased support to ceiling joists.

Hip roof detail.

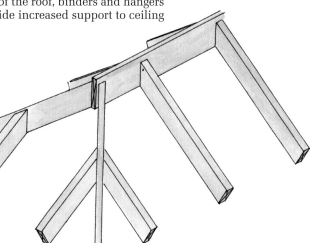

HIPPED ROOF

A hipped roof is where the roof is continuous around the building, as opposed to stopping at a gable end. Hip boards are attached to the wall plates at one end and the ridge board at the other. A wall plate will be attached to all the external walls of the extension off which the hipped roof will be built and braced across the corners to counter against spread. A hipped roof is far more complicated to construct than a close-coupled roof, with a large quantity of angles to cut. The smaller rafters between the hip boards and ridge board at one end and the valley boards and ridge board at the other end are called jack rafters. Covering a hipped roof also requires a greater degree of skill by the roof tiler, with both hip tiles and valley tiles adding to the need for accuracy during installation.

ROOF VALLEYS

Where a new pitched roof intersects an existing pitched roof at right angles, and part of the new roof is resting on the existing rafters, a valley will be formed. Valley boards, or layer boards, will be laid onto the existing rafters off which the new roof can be built. The existing roof timbers may need additional support to carry this extra load to be imposed upon it, and structural calculations may be required to prove that the support is sufficient. Where valleys are formed, weatherproofing is important as water enters the valleys from more than one slope. This open gutter can be lined with lead, copper or fibreglass, or purpose-made valley tiles can be used as valley liners.

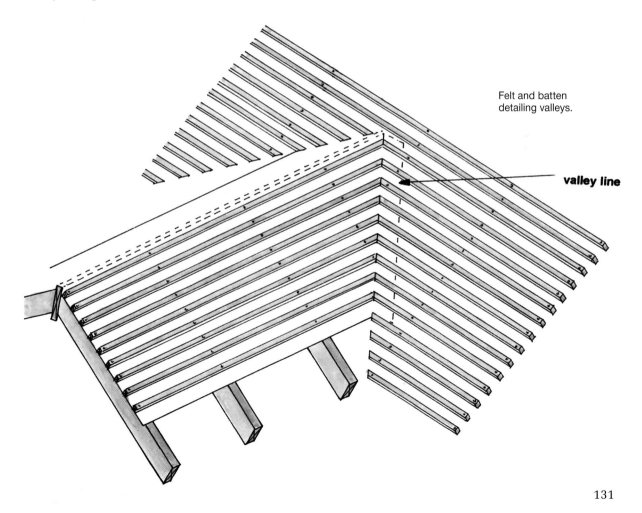

Felt and batten detailing valleys.

valley line

GABLE LADDER

Where the roof overlaps a gable end wall a support for the overhanging tiles will be needed. If the overhang is small, then a rafter on the outside of the wall structure may suffice. However, when the overhang exceeds 150 mm, then a gable ladder may be needed. Called a 'ladder' only because of its appearance, it will be made using the final internal rafter adjoining a similar rafter set externally. Bargeboards and soffits will provide the decorative covering.

FASCIA, SOFFIT AND BARGEBOARDS

The decorative timber facings around a roof's perimeter all fulfill a role. The vertical timber attached to the rafter ends along the eaves, providing both a good clean finish and an attachment for the guttering, is the fascia board. Set to 'kick up' the last line of tiles and to provide a drip over which water will run from the roof into the guttering, a fascia board can be found on the majority of modern homes built today.

Under (but attached to) the fascia is a soffit. The soffit closes off entrance to the roof void for birds and flying insects, yet provides ventilation, with soffit vents fitted at specified intervals. A soffit can be made in timber or masterboard-type materials. The bargeboards are the gable-end timbers running along the slope of the roof, providing a support for verge tiles overlapping the roof's edge. The fascia and bargeboards are commonly made from 25 mm thick timbers of varying widths.

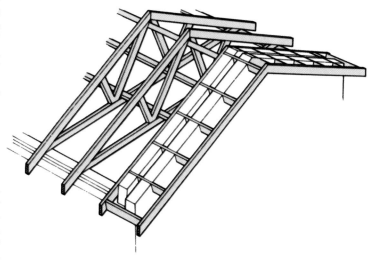

Gable ladder.

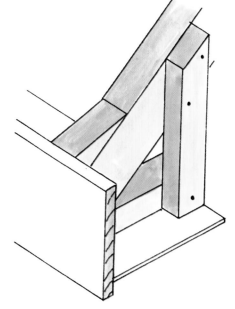

The vertical timber fascia board and horizontal soffit sheet.

FELT AND BATTEN

Roofing or sarking felt will provide a secondary protection to the roof area from wind-driven rain and snow. It should be untearable and suitable for this purpose. An overlap of at least 100 mm must be allowed where one layer joins another and secure joints around openings (soil vent pipes, for example) must be formed. The felt will be secured at eaves level and additional strips will be added to hip and valley areas.

Softwood roofing battens, treated with a preservative, will secure the roofing felt and where battens are joined the smallest battens should span at least three rafters. Batten sizes are generally 32 mm × 19 mm for rafters with up to 450 mm centres, and 32 mm × 25 mm for rafters with up to 600 mm centres. The nails or fixings used must be appropriate for this purpose.

Felt and batten showing hipped roof detail.

ROOF TILES

Pantiles, interlocking tiles and plain tiles form the majority of roof coverings in a huge variety of styles and colours. The plain tile, in clay and concrete, is slightly cambered to assist water discharge off the roof and into gutters. While tile-and-a-half tiles can be used at verges to provide staggered joints, eaves tiles will be used along the eaves to support the fall into the guttering and valley tiles are preformed and can be used to form the valleys. To finish off the hips and ridges, special tiles are available in a huge variety of shapes to complete the roof covering.

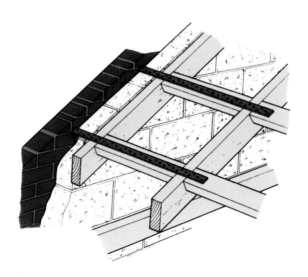

Vertical restraint straps.

Roofing

ROOF SLATES

Slates, natural and manufactured, are not as common as the clay and concrete tile but are still in use in most areas. The roofing slate will be secured by two, usually copper, nails with an overlap covering the nails. The first row of slates is then covered by the second row with a half-slate stagger, providing a half bond to reduce wind damage to what is quite a light roof and to ensure a watertight finish.

Ridges and hips are often made from clay, of a different colour to the roof slates, providing a clear outline to the roof.

CROSS-VENTILATION

Condensation is as important within a pitched roof as it is in a flat roof. Roof voids provide the perfect opportunity for condensation to cause problems in well-insulated and energy-efficient modern buildings. For this reason, building regulations stipulate that sufficient ventilation of the roof void must be provided. The normal method of roof ventilation is to provide continuous eaves ventilation, equivalent to a 10 mm gap along the total eaves length, along opposite sides of the building to provide an unobstructed airflow above the insulated ceiling. Roof and rafter ventilators are available to assist a free flow of air over the insulation quilt laid at the eaves. Airbricks built into gable walls at a high level will provide alternatives for lean-to roofs or roofs where eaves ventilation in opposite walls is not possible. Special channels and soffit vents can be built into roofs at eaves level to support the continuous flow of air over the insulation without blocking roof ventilation.

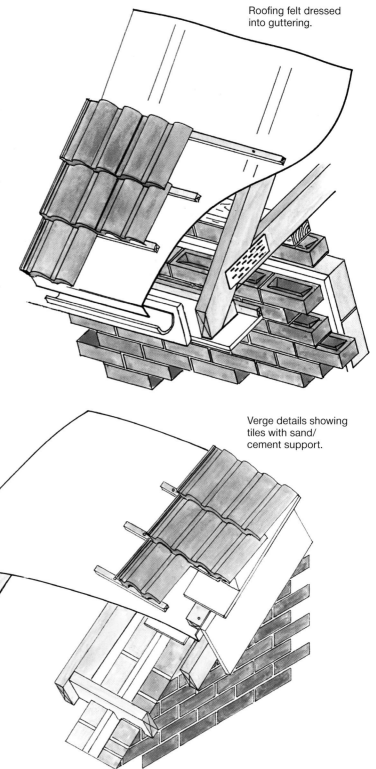

Roofing felt dressed into guttering.

Verge details showing tiles with sand/cement support.

CAVITY TRAY

Water penetrating walls as a result of heavy or driving rain, for example, can travel through to the inner wall of a building, resulting in unwanted damp patches. To prevent this from occurring, a cavity tray must be installed. Lintels over windows and doors now have a built-in cavity tray but in other areas where an external wall becomes an internal wall, in an extension for example, damp must not be allowed to travel down the cavity and enter the building. A cavity tray will prevent this and divert any water that has penetrated the outer wall back out through weep holes in the outer wall. Where a cavity tray is required above a flat roof, install it before the built-up felt is laid. Using the roof decking for support, you will need to remove a course of bricks, three or four at a time, to insert the cavity tray according to the manufacturer's instructions. Weep holes will be left in the mortar joints at regular intervals to let any water in the cavity escape.

LEAD FLASHING

Where a felt roof abuts a wall, against the existing house perhaps, the mineral felt must be dressed up the wall and into a chased-out mortar joint, then re-bedded in mortar. To complete the protection of this joint a lead flashing can be dressed down over it to finish not closer than 75 mm off the roof surface. When a cavity tray is installed it should discharge any moisture from the cavity out over the flashing. This will complete the protection of a vulnerable area where water penetration can be a problem if the process is not carried out in sequence and to a good building standard. The lead flashing specifications will be indicated on your building plans.

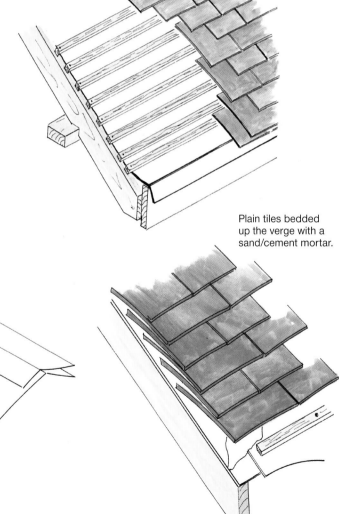

Plain tiles with eaves tiles along the eaves.

Plain tiles bedded up the verge with a sand/cement mortar.

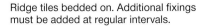

Ridge tiles bedded on. Additional fixings must be added at regular intervals.

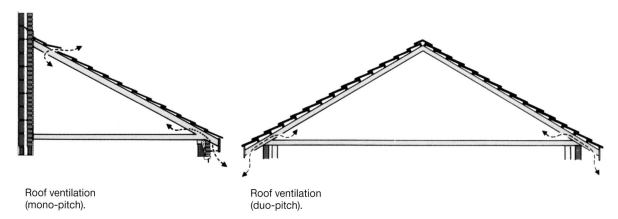

Roof ventilation
(mono-pitch).

Roof ventilation
(duo-pitch).

GUTTERING

While the scaffolding is still *in situ* and
when the roof covering is completed the
rainwater guttering can be fitted. There
are a wide variety of styles and colours
in cast iron, plastic and aluminium
to choose from but it is likely that you
will use a gutter identical to the existing
property. Gutter brackets should be set
at approximately 900 mm centres, under
standard domestic conditions, and down-
pipe brackets set at 2 m centres. These
measurements are for guidance purposes
only. It is worth noting that this may be
a good time to decorate the fascia boards
and other timbers, off the scaffolding
and before the gutters are fitted. Good
planning at this stage will save both time
and money later on.

Where a carpenter is to be employed,
try to get a price for the complete project,
as opposed to each individual part of the
project. However, only pay for the work
that is completed and not for work yet to
be completed.

CARPENTRY

Building a pitched roof on site is not a
job for the inexperienced. Always use
the most experienced tradesman you can
find, as any extra cost is likely to
be offset by the quality of the
finished product. Snug-
fitting joints at ridge and
eaves and bird's mouth
fitting at wall plate level,
not to mention the addi-
tional work involved with
a hipped roof, will not only
add to the strength and stability
of the roof structure, it will almost
certainly show through when the roof
is finished.

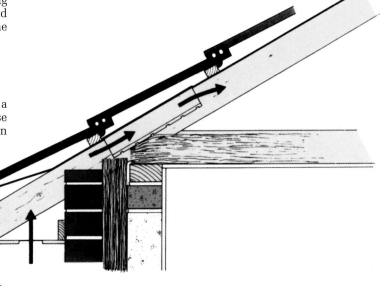

Eaves ventilation.

GETTING QUOTATIONS

The carpenter, as with some of the other tradesmen, will quote to do the work by one of two methods. The first, and the most common, is 'price work'. From the drawings a price to complete the work will be submitted for your acceptance. It may be broken down into phases of, say, the roof, the flooring and the finishings or it may be a total, completed price. The work will not include bedding on the wall plates (the bricklayer is responsible for this) but it will include, unless otherwise specified, stripping the back tiles where a new roof abutts an existing roof, for valleys to be formed and so on, and the fitting of fascias and soffits. The carpenter may also be the best person to fit the guttering, though this will not generally be included in the price given.

Second, the carpenter can work on a 'day rate' basis. This is commonly used for standard smaller domestic projects where the work, especially conversion work, is difficult to price. On a day rate basis the carpenter will agree a price per day, and the work to be carried out on this basis. Unless otherwise agreed the carpenter will then expect to be paid at the end of each week.

Other tradesmen from whom quotations may be required will be roof tilers and flat roof contractors. These two trades will differ in their requirements. A roof tiler may work on a price work or a day rate basis and may even agree to 'supply and fix'. The flat roofer will work on a price work, supply-and-fix basis.

Tiles and roofing felt dressed into guttering.

Mild steel restraint straps securing trusses to the gable wall.

Roofing

The larger roof tiling businesses often work on supply-and-fix rates. This method may seem expensive but it will reduce the risk of over-ordering and wastage. It is not unusual, in these instances, for a small deposit to be requested for the materials. If you are quite happy to supply all the materials, then a labour-only price is what you want. The price will include laying all felt, battens and tiles, forming valleys and bedding verge and ridge tiles. Unless specified in the price it is unlikely to include installing lead valleys or fixing lead flashings. For small projects, including garage conversions, this work should be carried out on a price work basis: one payment when the roof is complete.

FIRST FIX

When the roof structure is complete and the building shell is 'in the dry', then attention can be given to the 'finishing off' trades. These will include plastering, electrical work and plumbing. Before any of these trades can start their first fix, all the internal walls not built at the same time as the external walls, those forming individual rooms, will need to be built and positioned ready to be plaster-skimmed or dry-lined.

Walls can be built prior to the fitting of the ceiling boards, though it may be simpler to board the ceiling before the internal walls are built. The limited nature of a garage conversion may well restrict the movement of large sheet materials and this will include ceiling boards. Where walls run in the same direction as the ceiling joists, then noggins will be required to ensure wall stability and provide a suitable fixing point.

INTERNAL LOAD-BEARING WALLS

Often, smaller conversion works will only have enough room to produce one suitable habitable space, a dining room or a bedroom perhaps. But in cases where more than one room is planned, then an internal wall will be built. The wall will be a 'load-bearing' wall if it is included in the building calculations and is taken into consideration as a supporting wall for floor or roof joists.

This does not automatically mean that when joists pass directly over a wall it will be load-bearing. The joists in question may be able to span from one wall to another without requiring support from the intermediate wall it passes over. A load-bearing wall will be shown as such on the approved building plans and will be built off a proper foundation excavated along with the other foundations and built up with all the other walls to damp course level, and so on. In many cases the wall may be built using lightweight blocks but if it is load-bearing it will still need a foundation support. Where the support is limited, then simply increasing the depth of oversite concrete directly beneath this wall may suffice. As with any external wall any openings for doors or windows in a load-bearing wall will require a lintel installed to building regulations requirements.

INTERNAL NON-LOAD-BEARING WALLS

Unlike load-bearing walls, non-load-bearing walls do not need to be built off a proper foundation. There will not be any load imposed onto this wall; it will be free-standing and can be built off the oversite concrete, or with a timber floor it can be built off double joists. The choice of materials you can use for a non-load-bearing wall will be, commonly, either timber studwork or lightweight blocks. The use of heavier materials will increase the risk of additional foundations being required. For example, building a solid concrete block wall directly onto the concrete oversite will provide a 'point' load that will almost certainly be unacceptable to Building Control.

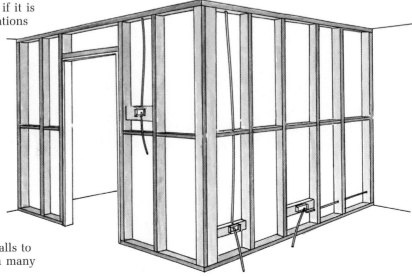

Stud partition with electricity cables in place.

Lightweight blocks will be perfectly adequate and will provide a very solid wall. However, even with lightweight blocks you may be required to thicken the oversite area a little to accommodate the extra load imposed upon it. A good alternative to lightweight blocks is timber studwork.

STUDWORK WALLS

The design and use of timber stud partition walls, particularly at first-floor level, has been transformed owing to the extensive use of truss rafters in modern house-building. At one time all internal walls were load-bearing, with the first-floor walls built in brickwork or blockwork directly above the ground-floor walls and thus carrying the roof load. The job of carrying the roof load has now been taken on by the truss rafters, which are designed to span between the opposite external walls of a building, allowing for any first-floor partitions to be simply room dividers. As a consequence architects and designers, allowed a free choice of wall position, regularly specify the use of lightweight stud partitions and core-filled partitions when they are planning first-floor constructions. The same will apply with conversion work where the walls are to be non-load-bearing partition walls. The lightweight stud partition wall is constructed in softwood, often using 100 mm × 50 mm sawn timbers with a plasterboard skin on either side. To reduce sound travelling through the partition (when used for bathrooms and toilets, for example) the cavity between the two plasterboard skins can be filled with mineral wool slabs or a glass fibre quilt.

To build a stud partition you must first set out the wall positions on the floor and ceiling. Then, following the lines marked out, two horizontal timbers acting as a base plate on the floor and a header plate on the ceiling can be fixed. The first, the base plate, is nailed to the flooring along the line of the proposed wall and the second, the header plate, following the same line, will be fixed to the ceiling. For added strength make sure you nail these timbers through the floorboarding and ceiling boarding directly into the floor and ceiling joists.

The vertical lengths of timber are called studs and can be erected and secured at 400 mm, 450 mm or 600 mm centres, as specified on the plans. The spacing of the studs will depend on the thickness of the plasterboard you use and the width of the boards. For 9.5 mm plasterboard the spacing should be no more than 450 mm, and for 12.55 mm plasterboard the spacing should be no more than 600 mm. Standard plasterboards are 1200 mm wide so the studs should be spaced to allow for the boards to join on a timber stud. As additional support and strength to the wall a third horizontal strip, called the noggins, will be added. The noggins will be cut down to fit about mid-height between the vertical studs to add rigidity to the framework and provide another fixing point for the plasterboards.

Door linings will be built into the structure before the plasterboard is added and any electrical cables or boxes and even central heating pipes must be installed before the walls are covered. All the services to be hidden within stud walls must be secured properly using the appropriate clips and checked to ensure there is no risk of leakage or short-circuiting. When the stud walls are completed they can be filled with a sound-deadening quilt, if required, and then covered with plasterboard sheets.

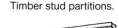

Timber stud partitions.

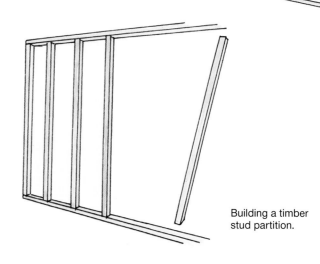

Building a timber stud partition.

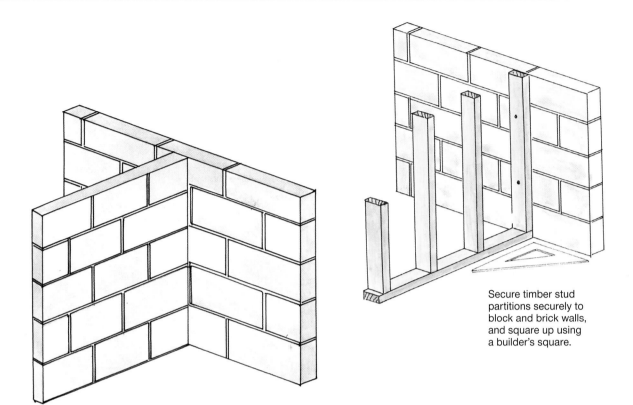

Secure timber stud partitions securely to block and brick walls, and square up using a builder's square.

Block partitions built into an external wall.

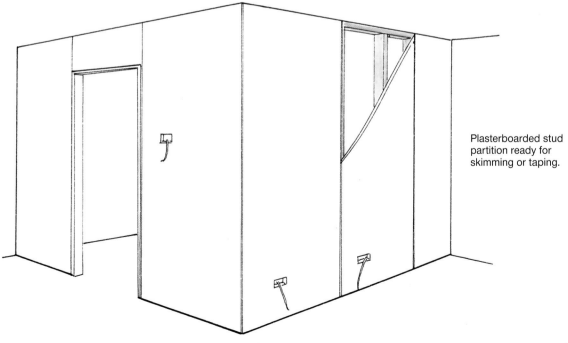

Plasterboarded stud partition ready for skimming or taping.

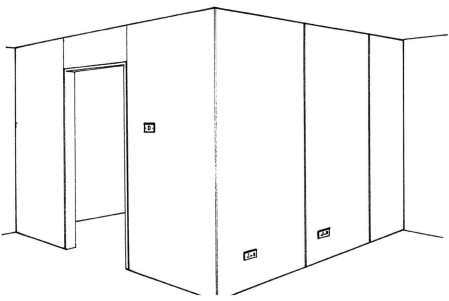

When the wall is ready for decoration the electrical points can be fitted.

As an added protection, usually to prevent or delay the spread of fire, plasterboards can also be fixed to studwork walls in double layers. The first layer will be nailed to the studs, then the second layer, fixed directly over the first layer but with the joints staggered to prevent a weak point, can be added.

LOFT HATCH

Access to the ceiling void through a trapdoor (more applicable for a pitched roof than a flat one) must be positioned correctly. The position of the access hatch, apart from being in a location where a loft-access ladder can be used, should be sensible without being overly prominent. The opening should be approximately 600 mm square, providing access to any water tanks or other services including access to insulate the roof. A loft hatch opening can be framed with trimmers in a 'cut' rafter roof but should be sized to suit the spacing available in a truss rafter roof.

Rebated 'linings' for the hatchway will be fitted with stops, similar to door linings and door stops, onto which the trapdoor will rest. The hatch lining should be set down, from the ceiling joists, the thickness of the ceiling boards so that a flush fit can be achieved.

For a flat roof, access to services such as electrical work and plumbing fittings may be necessary, so a small, concealed area should be provided at the appropriate point.

EXTERNAL DOORS

Doors can generally be divided into two categories: panel doors and flush doors. The panel door is made from hardwood or softwood with matching timber panels or rebated to receive glass panels, producing the required effect. A flush door will have an exterior grade plywood finish over a filled core and will occasionally have openings for glass panels. With so many doors from which to choose and such a wide range of suppliers, any selection you make will be down to personal choice or simply to match existing doors.

Hanging a new door into a new frame may require a little adjustment but hanging a new door into an old frame is not recommended. If at all possible install both a new frame and a new door. Try to make sure the door you select suits the frame. For example, a hardwood door will complement a hardwood frame and a painted door will complement a painted frame. The choice of door furniture is also extensive and again will be based on personal choice.

MADE-TO-MEASURE WINDOWS

A made-to-measure window is exactly what it says: a window made specifically for the opening available for it, and not a standard window of a given size, available from the multitude of manufacturers.

The selection process to use when selecting both windows and doors will be guided, inevitably, by the windows and doors used on the existing property and, although the planning authority may not be required to pass judgement on your choice, they will be keen for you to keep to a regular theme (and in particular not to become shocking or exhibitionist). In the window market there is not only a range of styles from which to choose, including top hung, sash, Georgian and so on, there are also several types of material, including uPVC, aluminium, hardwood and pine.

Window and door installation should be left until the walls are complete and the building is watertight. With the building tradesmen out of the way the possibility of damage to these expensive items is greatly reduced. After the windows and doors have been installed the window boards and door cills can be added in readiness for the plastering and floor screeding.

At the building stage do remember that it is very important to make sure that the window and door sizes are supplied by the manufacturer so that accurate templates can be made for the bricklayer to use.

GLAZING

Glass has been around for several centuries, becoming increasingly effective during the sixteenth century in Venice when molten glass was spun into a flat dish shape, then cut into rectangles. Clear plate glass, however, wasn't introduced until the nineteenth century and it wasn't until as recently as the 1950s that a certain Pilkington Brothers of England perfected float glass. Float glass is the most common type of glass used for domestic fittings and comes in a variety of thicknesses, from 4 mm upwards.

The thickness of glass required for your windows will depend very much upon the size of the opening and how far from the floor the opening is situated. For glass door panels, side panels and windows within 800 mm of the floor level the glass must be of a quality which, if broken on impact, is unlikely to cause injury, such as toughened or laminated safety glass. The size of the opening will also govern the thickness of the glass required, while in bathrooms and toilets obscure glass should be fitted.

Before fixing glass into a wooden frame make sure that the rebate is cleaned, undercoated and painted with an oil-based paint. The rebate can then be puttied along the inner edge prior to the glass being fitted and held in place with small headless nails. The open rebate can then be puttied and finished off tidily. Glass in door panels will be held in place using glazing sealant and wooden glazing beads.

Fixing glass into a metal frame is a similar process where the rebates will be painted with an appropriate frame paint and the glass fitted as with a wooden frame, except that clips instead of nails will secure the glass.

THE GLAZIER

Unless you are a really keen DIY'er and you find installing glass to be a fairly simple task, there are few other reasons for not using a glazier. The glazier will supply and fix the glass you require, saving both time and money and eliminating wastage.

DOUBLE GLAZING

The are two types of double-glazed window units: primary and secondary double glazing. Primary double glazing is where two panes of glass are hermetically sealed together with a clear gap between them to form a 'sealed unit' and this is then fitted into the rebated window frame as one unit. Secondary double glazing is where the existing window has a separate and independent pane of glass fitted over it.

It is important that, when ordering window frames, they have sufficient rebate to receive the double-glazed sealed units and are suitable for your purpose.

DOOR LININGS

Unlike door frames, softwood door linings are for internal doors and consist of two jambs and a head with loose doorstops. The doorstops can be positioned when the door is hung to produce an appropriate rebate for the door, ensuring a snug fit.

Door linings are available in a variety of sizes, all relevant to the thickness of the partition walls into which the linings are to be built. Frame ties should be used when fixing a door lining into a block partition wall and screws or nails should be used when fixing the lining into timber partitions.

If the linings are to be stained or varnished rather than painted, be sure to cover the frame before it is exposed to mortar or it will stain badly. Door linings can be ordered already assembled or they can be built on site when required.

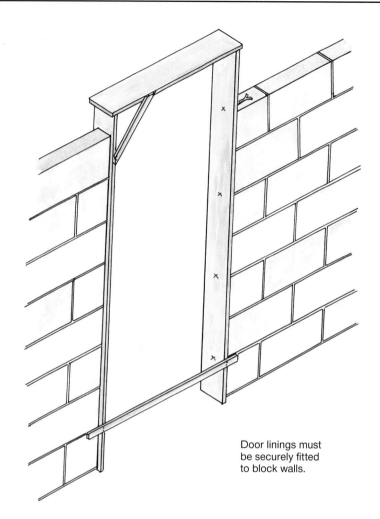

Door linings must be securely fitted to block walls.

FIRST FIX: ELECTRICS

The installation of electrical fittings no longer falls into the DIY category as this work must now be carried out by an approved domestic contractor, or inspected and certified by an approved domestic contractor. The National Inspection Council for Electrical Installation Contracting will have a list of approved domestic contractors within your area. Building Control will no longer allow the work to be carried out by the unskilled or unapproved.

For guidance the points of good practice and good installation have been laid out in a hefty tome called *Wiring Regulations*, which is produced by the Institute of Electrical Engineers.

In England and Wales domestic installations are usually supplied directly from a small local substation where the power into the substation is reduced for domestic use into a 240-volt single-phase supply. It is then cabled into homes underground or overhead where the supply is run through a meter before it is connected to the fuseboard. At the fuseboard, fuses, or circuit breakers, are fitted as a precaution against overloading and short-circuiting the supply. At the fuseboard the supply will be separated into fused sections and each fused section will serve individual facilities such as the cooker and the water heater. Power points or plug sockets will have at least two fused sections, as will the lighting circuits.

Overloading the fuseboard can be the result of using an appliance connected to a lower current supply and short-circuiting can occur when the live wire touches either the neutral or the earth wires. To reduce electric shocks there is now a strict 'earthing' method for each system. In older properties the electricity system would have been earthed simply by connection to the water pipes and, although little has changed, there is now a much more sophisticated earthing process in use.

The demands placed upon modern electricity supplies today are due to the number of accessories now available to connect to it, and it requires the services of only qualified electricians to make additions or alterations. The electrician will discuss your requirements with you and he will need to inspect your incoming supply plus the existing fuseboard before a quotation can be given. Larger additions can place quite a demand on the existing fittings and, when this is the case, a new fuseboard may be required. Caution with electrical installations must be observed at all times. This is not an area where penny-pinching can be considered.

Make sure the electrician is qualified, a member of the National Inspection Council for Electrical Installation Contracting and make sure you get more than one quote. When you have selected your electrician the first job will be to fix and position the cables and boxes, known in the trade as a 'first fix', so that the ceilings can be boarded and the walls can be plastered. After the cables and boxes are fixed in position and the light fitting cables secured, take a good look at the layout and double-check your requirements. If you want to add plug sockets or light fittings, now is the time, before the plastering starts.

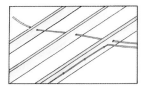

Electricity cables must be secured and positioned out of harm's way.

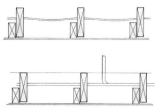

Cables and pipes must be set to a depth out of reach from nails and screws.

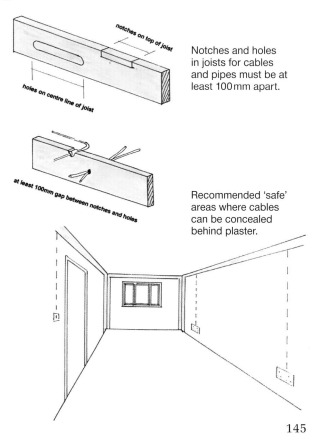

Notches and holes in joists for cables and pipes must be at least 100mm apart.

Recommended 'safe' areas where cables can be concealed behind plaster.

FIRST FIX: PLUMBING

There are two areas where plumbing may be required for your conversion. The first is the addition of radiators for central heating and the second is to supply water for sinks, baths or toilets. The plumber will want to view your existing facilities before an accurate quotation can be given. Adding radiators to an existing system may put excessive demands upon the existing water heater, thus reducing its ability to heat the home properly. If this is the case a new water heater may be required.

Plumbing is a skilled trade and only approved installers should be used. A very well-known regulatory body such as CORGI will assist you when selecting your plumber and this is vital if any of the work involves the gas supply.

The addition of a water supply for new facilities (such as a sink or a toilet) from the mains should be quite a straightforward installation, with the cold water supply to the sink coming directly from the mains supply. The cold water supply for baths and toilets can be from a cold water tank in the loft. Hot water will be supplied from the existing or a newly installed hot water tank.

Where the pipes to these facilities are required to be hidden behind ceilings or in floors, make sure you mark their location on your building plans for future reference. If the pipes are to be visible, the installation of surface-mounted pipes and their fixing will be carried out after the walls have been completed and prior to decorating.

Plumbing is clearly one of the areas where the DIY enthusiast has been targeted and pampered. The materials used and the layout of many systems are designed to help where experience falls short. There are, though, still areas where the enthusiast must seek professional assistance and installing a new gas boiler or a new hot water tank are just two such specialist areas. Adding radiators to an existing system and even adding bathing and toilet facilities should hold few terrors for the keen DIY enthusiast. There is, however, one simple note of caution: if you lack experience in jointing copper pipes, you may find that concealing them in ceilings and under floors before the system is checked and found to be watertight could result in expensive problems.

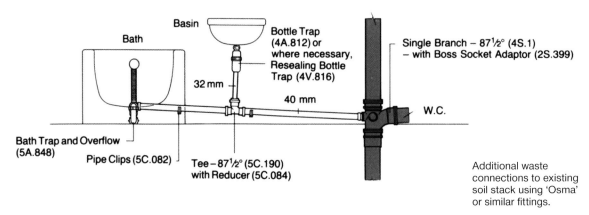

Additional waste connections to existing soil stack using 'Osma' or similar fittings.

CEILING BOARDS

The decorative finish you want to achieve for the ceilings will determine what materials are used. The most popular material, very widely used in modern building construction, is plasterboard sheets with a choice of Artex or plaster skim to provide the finish. Plasterboards are excellent for ceilings with an ivory-coloured finish side suitable for either direct decoration or for plaster skimming.

The boards are filled with a gypsum plaster core and should be secured in place using self-tapping screws. When the boards are in place and secure the joints can be taped where the ceilings are painted or can be muslin-jointed prior to plaster skimming.

Plasterboards are available in a variety of sizes, although 2400 mm × 1200 mm is the most common, and the thickness of the board you use will be determined by the span between the ceiling joists. Where joists have centres of up to 450 mm, then 9.55 mm boards are acceptable, and where the joists are centred up to 600 mm, then 12.5 mm boards will be preferable.

FIRE RESISTANCE

Plasterboards provide an excellent fire resistance for domestic situations, protecting the timbers and reducing or delaying the spread of the fire. The plasterboards should be fixed lengthways at right angles to the joists and the ends must meet on a joist. For additional fire protection to structural elements at risk, the plasterboard can be doubled up with a second layer and the joints staggered to provide continued protection. When the boards are fitted, the joints will be taped and the edges will be sealed along the walls to provide fire and fume protection.

LOFT INSULATION

To reduce heat loss from your home by up to 25 per cent the loft space must be insulated to comply with Approved Document L of building regulations. Available in either loose-fill, solid-board or blanket quilt, the insulation should be a minimum of 100 mm in depth and must cover the complete loft area.

Loose-fill insulation is available as mineral fibre or vermiculite particles and can be poured between the joists, using a rake to level off. Loose fill is particularly ideal for areas where access is limited or for pouring into areas where sound insulation is required, for example between floors and ceilings. The advantages of loose fill insulation are that there is no cutting, it is non-combustible and does not leave gaps.

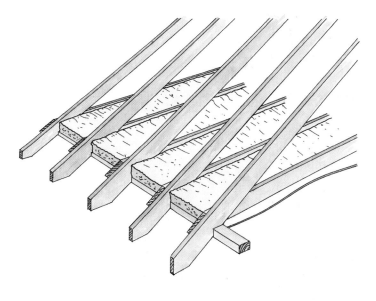

Loft insulation must be taken to the eaves.

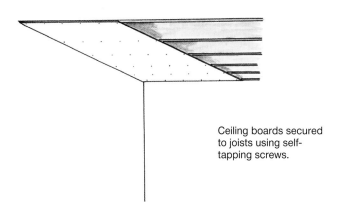

Ceiling boards secured to joists using self-tapping screws.

Quilt insulation is available in rolls and can be cut easily to size to suit the joist centres. The installation is relatively simple, though gloves and masks should be worn at all times. The quilt can be laid tightly between the joists and tucked into the eaves; make sure to allow for ventilation at eaves level. The advantages of quilt insulation are that it is likely to be cheaper than loose fill, it is also non-combustible and it is easy to cut.

Both loose-fill and quilt insulation should not rot, should inhibit fungal, mould and bacterial growth and should be vermin-proof. Insulation specifications will be clearly indicated on the approved plans and any alterations to this must be approved with the building inspector prior to the work being carried out.

SECOND FIX: ELECTRICS

To complete the contract, the electrician will return, when instructed, to add socket and light fittings to the cables fixed earlier in the project. The second fixing will be dependent upon the finishes being planned for walls and ceilings. Ceiling roses, for light fittings, should be fixed *before* the ceiling is Artexed but *after* the ceiling is plaster-skimmed. The process of adding fittings is fairly quick and when the circuits have been tested, then the job is finished.

There is a wide range of fittings and fixtures on the market but it is preferable that the majority will complement the existing fittings. Any changes should be discussed with the electrician at the quotation stage, or at least before the second fix is completed. It may not be too late to add sockets or lights but there will be a lot of extra and repair work to be carried out if you do. Getting it right at the first fix stage is very important.

SECOND FIX: PLUMBING

Second-fix plumbing may require more work than is required for the electrical fittings, though the process is rather similar. Fixing radiators will be done after the walls have been plastered and, with careful planning, after the walls have been decorated. Painting behind a radiator can be rather tiresome, so if you have selected the materials you plan to use and the colours, then this may well be a good time to paint those awkward areas.

Fixing washing and toilet facilities will also be carried out after the walls have been plastered. All of these facilities can be tested before the plumber leaves the site but small leaks are not uncommon within the first few days of use, so contact with the plumber should be maintained for future needs.

STEP-BY-STEP SUMMARY

1. Build all internal walls and fix door linings in place.
2. Form loft hatch in pitched roofs to allow access for services and insulating.
3. Fit all external doors and double-glazed units. Where the windows are glazed, this can now be carried out.
4. When the building is 'in the dry', first-fix electricity and plumbing can be addressed.
5. When the cables and pipes are in place the ceiling boards can be screwed in using self-tapping screws. Loft insulation can be added when the ceiling boards are fitted.
6. Second-fix electricity and plumbing works can be completed.

ELECTRICS
All electrical works must be carried out by an approved contractor. The National Inspection Council for Electrical Installation Contracting will have a list of local registered contractors.

PLUMBING
Adding to the existing system may not be within the scope of the existing boiler. Where a new gas boiler is required, make sure the installer is CORGI registered.

POINT OF GOOD BUILDING PRACTICE 10
In all new work consideration must be given to the inclusion of smoke detectors. Where applicable the new smoke detectors will be included on an independent electrical circuit.

FINISHING OFF

Both the building structure and the aesthetic appearance of the modern domestic dwelling has developed because of the demands placed upon designers and architects to conserve energy and to provide adequate accommodation for the twentieth-century family within an ever-reducing space. The internal finishes and furnishings, however, appear to be going in a totally different direction, seeking a style long past.

With both Tudor and Elizabethan designs and room layouts admired as 'the way to go', and with antique furniture and trinkets adorning more and more modern homes, the overall picture of progress is becoming confused. The desire to live comfortably has been accompanied by the equally strong desire to display one's wealth, and this is likely to be a result of the housing revolution in the 1970s. To confuse the picture even more you will find that not all rooms are heading in the same direction. The bathroom styles of the 1960s, 1970s and 1980s are being constantly scorned by designers who are extolling the virtues of pre-war fixtures and fittings. Kitchens are taking a similar route: after a drive toward the use of timber board sheets, including MDF and chipboard, the demand for all-wood kitchens is growing.

On a very positive note this adds both colour and splendour to our homes as we are at the beginning of a new century. It can only be considered a definitive move and a testament to past generations that their styles are popular and much sought-after. This emphasis on self-selection permeates a complete range of possibilities, where even the smallest of homes can now reflect a range of choices never before seen in home design.

The style of the new conversion work may encompass all these possibilities, or it may simply be an addition to meet increasing needs. Whatever the outcome and the choice of design or decoration, the structural preparations will be the same and must have been followed carefully to provide a base from which you can achieve only the best possible results.

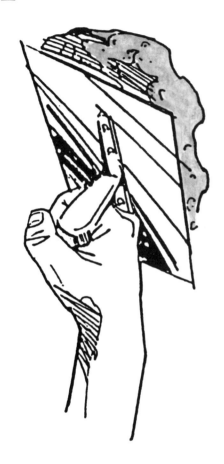

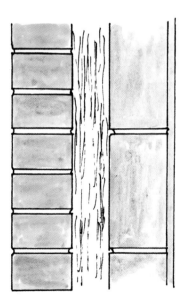

Fully insulated cavity wall with plaster- and skim-finish.

PLASTERING AND SKIMMING

Apart from decorative stone walling and the occasional brick fireplace we do prefer the majority of our internal walls to be either painted or wall-papered. To provide a suitable surface for these decorating processes the internal walls will be covered with at least two coats of plaster: a base coat to cover the rough surface of the building blocks and a smooth skim coat to finish. Plastering is definitely a highly skilled trade that requires both speed and accuracy.

The first coat, called the floating coat, is applied using a hawk and trowel to a depth of between 10 mm and 13 mm over the wall. A straight-edge will be used to provide a level and even surface, then a special tool called a 'devilled' float is dragged over the surface of the plaster to provide a key for the finishing coat. The 'devilled' float or trowel has sharp points and provides a gauged effect on the surface of the floating coat of plaster. The base coat will then be allowed to set but not dry out completely (leave for about two hours); then you can apply the smooth finishing coat using a float and brush. The brush is used to flick water onto the plaster surface, which, when the float is used, produces a hard shiny finish. If the base coat gets too dry it may require dampening before the skim coat can be applied.

Where internal studwork walls are plasterboarded to be plaster-skim finished, to provide a smooth finish the plaster skim coat will be applied after the plasterboard joints have been taped or scrimmed. The drying-out process for this structure is very short indeed but the drying out of two-coat plaster walls will be much longer.

Electrical cables must be in place before the plastering commences but the fittings will be added after the walls are plastered. Never plaster near or around live electrical wires because the water involved with plastering can have fatal consequences.

ARTEXING

There are usually only two possible choices for the decoration of ceilings. The first is a plaster skim to be painted and the second, more popular in homes built in the last thirty years, is a white surface coat call Artex. This finish is not as popular as it used to be and is not as commonly used in new house-building.

To apply Artex to the ceiling boards the latter must be fixed with the ivory face downwards, to help the white Artex mixture provide a good crisp finish. The plasterboard joints are taped, Artex mixture is applied using a special brush and then before it is set a variety of finishes can be produced. These include a stipple-type finish and patterns of all kinds but your choice is likely to be the same as the finish used on your existing ceilings. It is reasonable to assume that the Artexer will copy your existing style unless he is otherwise directed. If you want to try something different, ask to see the different possible patterns before you go ahead. Unlike plastered ceilings where you can easily change the colour, Artexed ceilings are permanent.

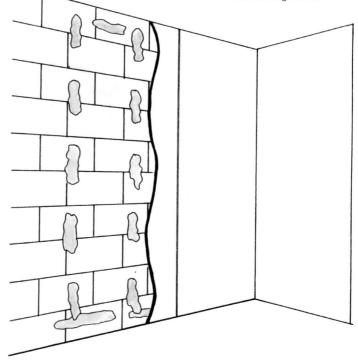

Dot-and-dab dry lining. The adhesive 'dabs' must provide a suitable support for the plasterboard and provide a fixing for the skirting board.

One other important point to remember is that the Artexer will be required *after* the electrician has secured the light fittings, whereas if your ceiling is being skimmed the plasterer will skim ceilings before the electrical fittings are in place.

DRY LINING

Dry lining is becoming more and more popular in domestic construction amongst some larger house builders because its faster drying-out period allows for earlier completions.

Dry-lined walls are an alternative to plastering. Plasterboards will be secured to the walls with either timber battens or, more commonly, plaster dabs. When the boards are secure the board joints will be taped and the walls are then ready for decoration, including wall-papering. The boards you use for dry-lining will have a tapered edge where the boards meet, and where a joint can be formed using a joint compound a joint tape will be bedded on and then given a slurry coat to finish.

This method is a popular alternative to wet plastering and it does have its benefits. It is clean, the boards can be decorated almost immediately and there is no shrinkage causing cracks. This process may be more expensive than plastering but it does add to the thermal qualities of the walls. If you do plan to dry-line the walls of your conversion you will need a specialist installer to carry out the work.

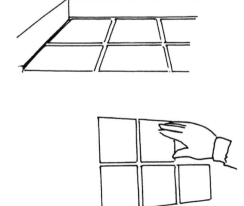

FLOOR TILING

Allow at least two weeks as a drying-out period before laying your floor tiles onto newly laid screed. Before laying your tiles – in fact before laying the floor screed – you must calculate where the finished floor level is to be. Then you can calculate the depth of floor screed required. The floor tiles can then be laid, as required and according to the manufacturer's specifications.

It is important to wait until the floor levels are established clearly before cutting any internal doors to size. Skirting boards or skirting tiles will provide the finished edgings and will be added when the floor tiles are down. If your floor includes a hidden manhole cover (inspection chamber lid), then this must also be installed to the finished floor level with the tiles bedded in the cover. The process of setting out the tiles should be carried out either from the manhole cover, if there is one, or from a line drawn centrally down the room and then adjusted slightly to reduce the number of cut tiles along the edges.

DRYING OUT

The drying-out process of a two-coat plaster wall will depend upon the moisture content of the walls being plastered and the atmospheric moisture. The plasterer will be the best person to advise how long the walls should be left before decoration. It is likely that a water-based paint, not a vinyl, will be best to use at first. Skimmed plasterboards on ceilings and stud partitions, on the other hand, are a much drier product and they will be ready for decoration within a very short period of time.

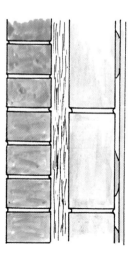

Fully insulated cavity wall with dry lining finish.

Finishing Off

The feeling of urgency to occupy your new building will be frustrated while this drying-out process is happening but do not try to dry out the building using heaters if it can possibly be avoided. The natural drying out or curing of water-based surfaces such as floor screeds and plastering provides a more secure and permanent surface, if they are allowed to dry at a sensible pace.

INTERNAL DOORS

The internal door, unlike its external counterpart, is commonly a very light-weight timber door fixed into a softwood door lining, hinged at one side allowing the door to open in the direction best suited for entry or exit. Choices can include single doors, double doors (where the opening is wider) and sliding doors or folding doors (where access may be limited).

The range of internal doors from which to choose includes flush doors, panelled doors, glazed doors and ledger and braced doors. With such a wide range from which to choose the purchaser is clearly spoiled for choice. Flush doors can have a hardwood veneer finish, removing the requirement for decorating, or have a plain timber finish to be decorated in the colour required. Panelled doors are also available in numerous styles, both pre-decorated and plain, or primed and ready for decoration. Glazed doors are heavier and rather more substantial, so require more attention when fixing. There are restrictions with glazed doors relevant to the type of glass used and at what height the glass panels are positioned. Accidents can occur with glazed doors so the glass type and strength must meet with all the necessary building requirements.

Finally, the ledger and braced door, of a heavy or a lightweight construction, is very much a country-style door and can be installed as a stable door where the top half and bottom half can open independently. This is popular but not necessarily ideal for privacy or sound-proofing.

The door selection you make will almost certainly depend upon the existing doors you have, though matching (especially with veneer doors) may be difficult. Whatever door style you choose,

you will have to fix door furniture. Again, like the doors, it is likely that your choice will reflect your existing door furniture, but, as with the doors themselves, the range is extensive. The choice will range from iron through aluminium to gold, with the possibilities being almost endless and the availability often almost instant. The hanging of the doors is not extremely difficult and should fall within the ability range of an experienced DIY'er, otherwise it is a job for the carpenter and is best carried out as the almost final part of the puzzle. Do not fix doors, except perhaps on a new bathroom, until the plasterer and plumber have finished.

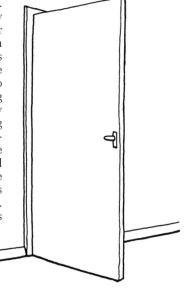

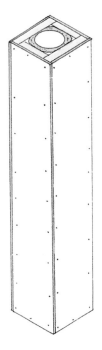
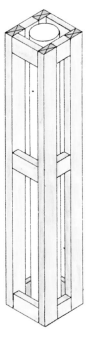

Where drainage pipes pass through habitable rooms they must be insulated to reduce noise and be boxed in for appearance.

SKIRTING BOARDS AND ARCHITRAVES

The decorative timbers used as an edge to door frames and walls are called skirting and architrave and are moulded strips of timber, cut to length and then secured to the door frame or wall using nails or screws. Mainly used for appearances, the skirting boards and architraves will hide the rough edges where the plastering reaches the flooring and abuts the door frame or door lining. There are various styles of both skirting and architrave from which to choose, with the most common being rounded and splayed, ogee or bull-nosed.

Skirting boards should be cut tightly into corners and jointed using mitred joints for appearance. They can be secured to the walls using cut nails, or can be drilled and screwed.

Around the door linings, two lengths of architrave will be cut as vertical lengths, one either side of the door, with a horizontal length above the door intersecting the verticals using a mitred 45-degree joint. Accuracy is fairly important, though filler can be added to conceal gaps where architraves are to be painted. A small margin should be left, around the lining, for appearance.

As a set, architraves and skirting are usually the same style, though skirting boards provide a different service. The architrave is purely for appearances whereas the skirting board acts as a dividing line between the floor and the walls, masking the joints between the plastering and the flooring and acting as a buffer to withstand knocks and bumps.

Skirting boards and architraves are usually sawn timbers to be primed, undercoated and glossed after fixing.

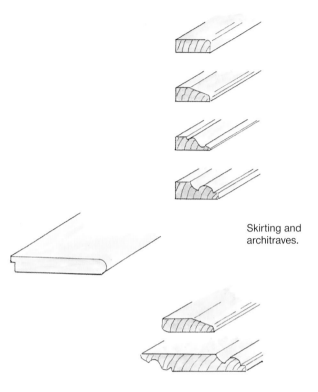

Skirting and architraves.

WALL TILING

Where the conversion work includes bathrooms, kitchens, toilets and utility rooms there may be areas where ceramic or similar wall tiles are to be added to guard against water damage to plastered surfaces. These tiles should be added after the plastering is completed and fixed according to the manufacturer's specifications.

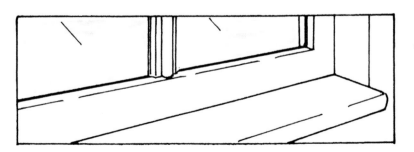

Window board fitted.

PAINTING AND DECORATING

Newly plastered walls beg to be decorated but a short drying-out process must be allowed before the brushes and rollers are used. Newly plastered walls can be decorated with a weak solution of emulsion paint, preferably not a vinyl, within a reasonable time of completion. Hanging wallpaper onto newly plastered walls, however, especially vinyl-type wallpapers, will prevent the drying-out process and should be avoided for several weeks, if not months after the work is completed. Skirting boards and architraves can be primed, undercoated and glossed before the walls and ceilings are painted.

Timber-framed walls and stud partitions finished with either a taped joint or a plaster skim can be decorated within days of completion because they require only a short drying-out period.

Window and door frames must have a mastic barrier added to finish.

TIDYING UP

When the building work is finally completed and all the rubbish has been removed from the site and taken to the local dump, there is likely to remain a small quantity of usable materials, including bricks and tiles. Some of this surplus you may not want to keep but spare bricks and tiles should be set aside in the unfortunate case of accidents occurring and identical replacements being required. How you dispose of the remaining items will depend upon your location, on the possibility of local builders looking to buy surplus items and on the materials themselves. Sand and ballast should not be too difficult to dispose of in the soakaway or somewhere around the garden; perhaps it can be used as a base for any paving slabs being added or replaced.

To tidy up the paperwork the Building Control officer should be notified that the work is now complete and your house insurance should be changed to include the new work. You can also complete the financial calculations that will help you to identify the total expenditure so that you can compare the figures with any quotations you obtained from local builders before the work started.

> **POINT OF GOOD BUILDING PRACTICE 11**
> Where rainwater is directed into a soakaway, the soakaway must be situated at least 5 m from all habitable buildings. At approximately 1 m³ in size the soakaway can be filled with non-perishable building materials such as broken bricks and blocks, then covered with a rigid sheet and at least 300 mm of soil.

1 cubic metre Soakaway
min. 5 metre from buildings
Hepworth 'Supersleeve'
pipes and couplings.

ADDRESS BOOK OF TRADESMEN

Full details of tradesmen used (for future reference).

Architect/Draughtsman
Name..........................
Address.......................
....
Tel. no..........................

Bricklayer
Name..........................
Address.......................
....
Tel. no. ....

Carpenter
Name..........................
Address.......................
....
Tel. no..........................

Felt roofer
Name..........................
Address.......................
....
Tel. no..........................

Roof tiler
Name..........................
Address.......................
....
Tel. no..........................

Electrician
Name..........................
Address.......................
....
Tel. no..........................

Plumber
Name..........................
Address.......................
....
Tel. no..........................

Glazier
Name........................
Address.....................
....
Tel. no........................

Scaffolder
Name..........................
Address.......................
....
Tel. no..........................

Plasterer
Name..........................
Address.......................
....
Tel. no..........................

Dry liner
Name..........................
Address.......................
....
Tel. no..........................

Artexer
Name..........................
Address.......................
....
Tel. no..........................

Painter/decorator
Name..........................
Address.......................
....
Tel. no..........................

USEFUL ADDRESSES

This shortlist of manufacturers and stockists has been assembled to help and guide you in any product selection you make when planning and building your new garage conversion. I would like to thank them for all the help they have given in the production of this book. If you have any questions about either the installation or availability of their products I am sure they will be happy provide you with all the information you require.

Concrete Blocks

Tarmac Topblock Ltd, Wolverhampton.
(01902) 754131
RMC Concrete Products Ltd, Buxton, Derbyshire.
(01298) 22244

Insulation Blocks

Thermalite Blocks, Marley Building Products, Sevenoaks, Kent.
(0990) 620900
H & H Celcon Blocks, Sevenoaks, Kent.
(01732) 880580

Drainage (Clay)

Naylor Clayware Ltd, Barnsley.
(01226) 790591
Hepworth Building Products, Sheffield.
(01226) 763561

Drainage (Plastic)

Polypipe plc, Doncaster.
(01709) 770000
Caradon Terrain Ltd. Aylesford, Kent.
(01622) 717811

Lintels

Dorman Long Ltd, British Steel Lintels, Newport, Gwent.
(01633) 244000
Caradon Catnic Ltd, Caerphilly, Wales.
(01222) 885955
Expamet Building Products, Hartlepool.
(01429) 866688

Bitumen Damp-Proof Membrane

Feb Ltd, Swinton, Manchester.
(0161 794) 7411

Insulating DPC

TDI (UK) Ltd, Matlock, Derbyshire.
(01629) 733177
Thermabate, RMC Products Ltd, Wakefield.
(01924) 362081

Roof Trusses

Gang Nail Systems Ltd, Aldershot, Hampshire.
(01252) 334562
Jewsons Builders Merchants, your local branch.
Wickes Building Supplies, your local branch

Roofing Felt

Monarflex, St Albans, Hertfordshire.
(01727) 830116

Roof Tiles

Marley Building Products, Sevenoaks, Kent.
(0990) 626900

Plasterboard

Lafarge Plasterboard, Bristol, Avon.
(01275) 375281

Cavity Insulation

Rockwool Ltd, Pencoed, Bridgend.
(01656) 862621
Kingspan, Leominster, Herefordshire.
(01544) 388601

Insulation Quilt

Superglass Insulation Ltd, Stirling, Scotland.
(01786) 451170

Floor Insulation

Kay-Metzler Ltd, Wickford, Essex.
(01268) 766301

Plumbing

Polypipe plc, Doncaster.
(01709) 770000

Rainwater Goods

Hunter Plastics Ltd, London, SE28.
(0181 855) 9851
Hepworth Building Products, Sheffield.
(01226) 763561

Tools: Spirit Levels

BMI Robust, see *www.brimarc.com*.

IMPORTANT CONTACTS

National House Building Council (NHBC)

Buildmark House
Chiltern Avenue
Amersham
Buckinghamshire
HP6 5AP
(0870) 2414302

Federation of Master Builders

Gordon Fisher House
14–15 Great James Street
London
WC1N 3DP
(0207) 2427583

**National Inspection Council for
Electrical Installation Contracting**

Warwick House
Houghton Hall Park
Houghton Regis
LU5 52X
(01582) 531000

The Council for Registered Gas Installers

'Corgi'
1 Elmwood
Chineham Park
Crockford Lane
Basingstoke
RG24 8WG
(0870) 4012200

INDEX

Access hatch 142
Aggregate 105
Airbricks 100, 102, 113, 134
Aircrete 105
Aluminium 110, 136, 143
Approved Document L 147
Architects 140
Architrave 153
Artex 147, 150
Asphalt 125

Back inlet gully 57
Bargeboards 132
Bathrooms 108
Battens 133
Beam and block 95, 104
Bitumen 99, 120, 125, 126,
Bitumen felt 124
Blockwork 140
Brackets 77
Bricklayer 90, 137
Brickwork 140
Building Control 88, 120, 139
Building inspector 96, 120
Building regulations 73, 89, 98,
106, 117, 119, 124, 134, 139

Carpenter 128, 136
Cast iron 136
Cavity bridging 78
Cavity closer 93
Cavity tray 135
Cavity wall 73
Cavity wall insulation 75
Ceiling boards 1243, 139
Cement 106
Central heating 108, 140, 146
Ceramic 153
Chalk lines 63
Chipboard 105, 116, 124
Chlorine 110
Circuit breakers 145
Clay ducting 102
Clay tiles 127, 133
Cold roof 120, 125
Cold water tank 146
Concrete block 95, 105
Concrete floor 95
Concrete slab 95
Concrete tiles 130, 134
Condensation 92, 120, 122, 127, 134
Contamination 104
Copper 131
Copper nails 134
CORGI 146
Cross ventilation 122

Damp 135
Damp-proof course 63, 96, 113
Damp-proof membrane 98, 102, 106

Datum levels 63
Datum peg 63
Day rate 86, 137
Decking 116, 120, 122, 124, 135
Designers 107, 140
'Devilled' float 150
Door cill 93
Door furniture 142
Door linings 140
Double glazing 144
Double joists 115, 139
Double-sealed cover 54
Dry lining 151
Dry rot 106

Eaves 122
Eaves tiles 133
Eaves ventilation 134
Electrical cables 140
Electrical work 139
Electrician 145
Elizabethan 149
Emulsion 154
Energy conservation 127

Fascia 132, 136, 137
Felt 138
Felt roof 121
Felt roof contractors 156
Fibreglass 131
Fire 142, 147
Fire safety 89
Firring piece 124
Flat roof 114, 119, 120, 124,
142
Floating floor 105
Floor joists 113
Floorboards 116
Foul waste 49, 115
Foundations 73, 139
Frame ties 90, 94, 144
Frost 103
Fungal 106
Fungal growth 148
Fungi 100
Fuseboard 145

Gable end 131, 132
Gable ladder 132
Galvanized 90
Galvanized nails 121, 124, 125
Garage door 75
Gas boiler 146
Gas supply 146
Gauge rod 67
Georgian 143
Glass 140, 142
Glass fibre 140
Glazier 144
Glazing 108

Gloves 148
Gold 152
Guttering 136, 137
Gutters 124, 133
Gypsum 147

Hangers 130
Hardcore 97, 102, 104, 106
Hardwood 94, 142
Hardwood cill 94
Hawk 150
Heavy compactor 97
Herringbone 114
Hip boards 131
Hip tiles 131
Hipped roof 131, 136
Honeycomb 113
Hot water tank 146

Inspection chamber 53, 151
Insulation 96, 104, 112
Integral garage 38
Interior design 108
Iron 152

Jack rafters 131
JCB digger 61
Joint compound 151
Joists 121, 128

Kitchens 108

Laminated safety glass 143
Lead 131
Lead flashing 135
Lead valleys 138
Lean-to 130
Ledgers 87
Light fittings 145
Limescale 110
Limestone 125
Lintels 74, 135
Liquid membrane 96
Load bearing wall 139

Mains supply 146
Manhole 54
Mask 148
Masterboard 132
Mastic asphalt 125
Membrane 97, 99, 125
Mild steel restraint straps 121
Mineral felt 125, 126, 135
Mineral wool 140
Mortar 90, 144
Mould 92, 122
Muslin 147

Noggins 114, 115, 140
Non-hydraulic lime 78

Index

Oversite 97, 98, 99, 102, 103, 113, 139

Padstones 84
Panel doors 142
Pantiles 133
Partitions 140
Party wall 73
Paving slabs 154
Pea shingle 51
Perimeter walls 113
Pilkington Brothers 143
Pine 143
Plain tiles 133
Planning authority 143
Planning Department 120
Planning permission 74
Plasterboard 140, 147
Plastering 139, 143
Plastic 136
Plastic uPVC 51
Plasticizer 78
Plug sockets 145
Plumbing 139, 146
Plywood 116
Pole scaffolding 86
Polyethylene 110
Polystyrene 104
Polystyrene insulation 98
Polythene film 98
Portland cement 78
Power points 115, 145
Pre-mixed concrete 103
Pre-stressed concrete lintel 57
Price work 137, 138
Primer 90, 94
Profile boards 63
Public sewers 51
Purlins 130
Putlog 87

R-values 92
Radiators 108, 109, 115, 146
Raft foundation 68
Rafters 128, 130
Rainwater 124
Retarder 69
Ridge board 130
Ridge tiles 138
Roller door 77

Roof battens 133
Roof joists 139
Roof tiler 137
Roofing felt 133
RSJ's 74, 84

Sand 106
Sarking felt 133
Scaffolding 136
Screed 95, 105, 106, 151
Sealed units 144
Secondary double glazing 144
Self-tapping screws 116
Semi-hydraulic lime 78
Septic tank 51
Sewage 51
Sewage treatment plant 51
Shale 125
Sharp sand 97, 106
Side hung 88
Sink 146
Skirting board 151, 153
Skirting tiles 151
Slates 134
Sleeper walls 112
Slurry coat 151
Soffit 122, 132, 137
Soffit vents 132
Softwood 140
Soil vent pipe 133
Specifiers 107
Springs 76
Stainless steel 90
Standards 87
Steel plates 84
Stone 150
Stone chippings 126
Stonework 75
Structural calculations 131
Struts 114, 130
Stud partition 140
Studwork 139
Suspended floor 95, 100, 112, 113

Tanking 99
Tapered edge 151
Templates 90
Thermal bridging 92, 94
Thermal conductivity 92
Tilt fillet 125

Tilt windows 89
Timber frame 73
Toilet 146
Top-hung 89
Toughened glass 143
Tradesmen 137
Trickle vent 89
Triple joists 115
Trowel 78
Truss rafters 128, 140
Tudor 149

'U' values 78, 98
Ultraviolet 126
Undercoat 90, 94
Underfloor heating 106, 107
Underfoor ventilation 100
Underpinning 57, 60
Universal Beam 84
Up-and-over door 76
uPVC 93, 143
Utility room 153

Valley boards 131
Valley tiles 131
Vapour barrier 126
Vegetation 97
Ventilation 89, 96, 100, 102, 112, 134, 148
Ventilators 122
Verge tiles 138
Vermiculite 147
Vinyl 154
Vitrified clay 51

Wall plate 113, 120, 124, 128, 130
Wall ties 73
Wallpaper 154
Warm roof 120, 125
Waste disposal 49
Water bar 94
Waterproof membrane 126
Weedkiller 97
Weeds 97
Weep holes 135
Whacker plate 97
Window boards 143
Window frames 89
Wire mesh 106
Wood glue 116